AF491776

DR. THOMAS FLINT

BENJAMIN FLINT

LLEWELLYN BIXBY

[FROM DAGUERROTYPES TAKEN BETWEEN 1855 AND 1860]

The Diary of Dr. Thomas Flint

California to Maine and Return 1851-1855

Edited and with an Introduction by Gary Menchen

2024
pagesofpages.com
Waterville, Maine

Contact: editor@pagesofpages.com

The Diary and the Introduction by Waldemar Westergaard originally appeared in the *Annual Publication of the Historical Society of Southern California*, 1923, Vol. 12 No. 3, pp 53-127. The Notes by Sarah Bixby Smith were included at the end of a separate pamphlet publication of the diary, also identified as 1923.

Table of Contents

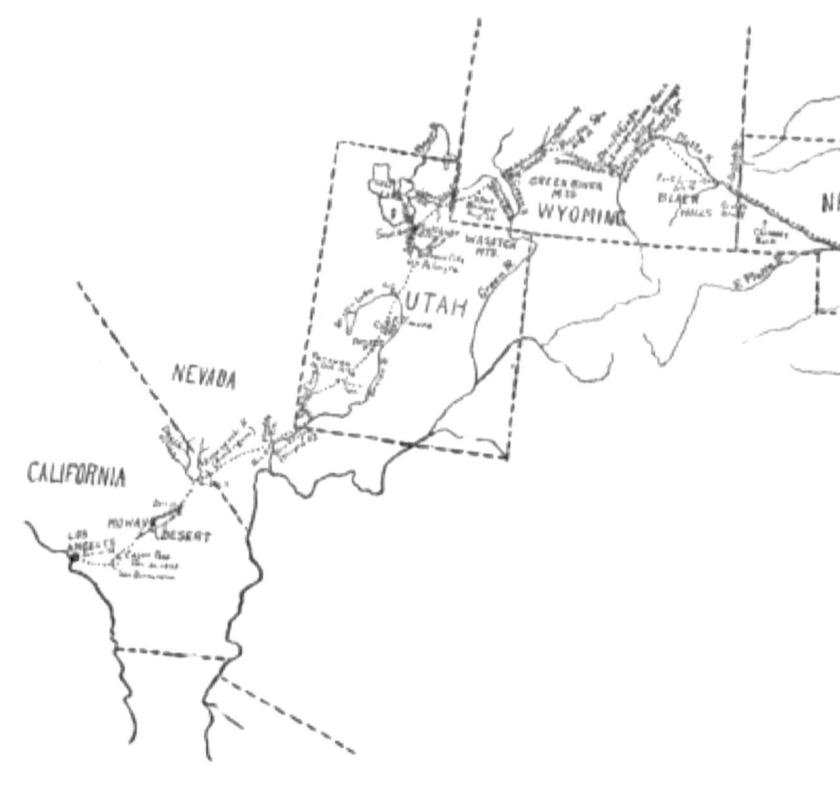
NE
WYOMING
GREEN RIVER MTS
BLACK
HILLS
UTAH
WASATCH MTS.
NEVADA
CALIFORNIA
MOHAVE DESERT
LOS ANGELES

Route of the FLINT-BIXBY Party 1853

Sketch Map to accompany the Diary of Dr. Thomas Flint

Introduction to This Edition

I first became aware of Thomas Flint while reading up on a once-notorious murder that occurred in Waterville, Maine in 1847. The case involved a physician., Valorous P. Coolidge, who was ultimately convicted of murder by lacing the drink of an acquaintance (who was carrying a good deal of cash) with prussic acid. One of his medical students, Thomas Flint, played a prominent in the trial accounts. Before a coroner's jury he knew nothing of the affair, but then turned witness for the trial, and admitted to helping hide the body of the victim. Flint was attacked by defense council as a perjurer and an accessory after the fact if he was telling the truth, was suspected by some of the public as the actual murderer, but was defended by the prosecution as a "mere boy"[1]

The "mere boy" was born May 13, 1824, and was 23 in late 1847, when the above murder occurred. Readers of this diary will, I believe, find him, a few years later, resolute and highly competent. He finished his medical education at Jefferson Medical College at Philadelphia in 1849, practiced in North Anson, Maine (where he had family) for a brief period, and then commenced this diary when he went west for the first time in 1851.

A few structural changes have been made to the original account, first published by the Historical Society of Southern

---

[1] For a collection of contemporary accounts of the case, and a detailed transcript of the trial, including Flint's testimony, see *The Trial of Dr. Valorus P. Coolidge and its Aftermath*, edited by Gary Menchen 2023.

California in 1923[2]. It has been broken into several chapters; minor spelling errors that did not seem characteristic of Flint have been corrected, and footnotes added. A few footnotes, ending in "[1923]" are from the 1923 edition.

---

[2] *Annual Publications of the Historical Society of California*, Vol XII, pt. III, 1923, pp. 53-127. Reprinted separately the same year, with Notes by Sarah Bixby Smith, 78p.

Introduction to the Edition of 1923

Of reminiscences dealing with the overland journey to California during the era of the Argonauts, there is no lack. When based on contemporary letters and documents, such reminiscences may, if used with discrimination by the investigator, have real historical value. Diaries kept from day to day by careful and conscientious observers are, it must be said, in quite a different class of historical literature. Human memory is so undependable a thing that unless observations have been made on the spot, important movements and personalities become rapidly hazy, and the researcher is correspondingly helpless.

The Diary of Dr. Thomas Flint gives a day-by-day picture of the actual life and experiences of a bright, observant young Maine Yankee during an exceedingly interesting period of Western American history. Our diarist was the first son of William Reed Flint and Electra Weston Flint, and was born in New Vineyard, Maine, on May 13, 1824. He died in San Juan Bautista, California, June 19, 1904. The first visit of Dr. Flint and his two cousins, Llewellyn and Amasa Bixby, was made in 1851, when they made the trip from Maine to the California gold fields by the Panama route. His brother had preceded him. The notes from this initial trip are comparatively brief, and the last entry connected with it was made July 12, the day of arrival at the Volcano Diggings in Amador county. The Diary is continued on Christmas Day, 1852, when Dr. Flint, with his brother Benjamin, and his first cousin, Llewellyn Bixby, leave the gold diggings for their round trip journey, which was to take them by water via Panama as before, to their New England home, 'uniting their fortunes, 'as they said, 'for the undertaking of bringing to California sheep and cattle. 'It is the story of this return trip, it is safe to say, that will interest students of California's past during the American period, and throw some light upon an interesting and romantic phase of the westward movement in American history. Certainly other parties that took the route of the "covered wagon "had more thrilling stories to tell than has Dr. Flint, whose party came through its ordeal remarkably well. Nevertheless, between the attacks or threatened depredations of wolves, bears, and red men, the physical difficulties encountered in bringing over 2,000 sheep, oxen, cows, and horses, over swollen streams, nearly impassible roads, vast stretches of desert where water, if found at all, was too brackish for even the beasts to drink, the story here revealed will perhaps seem to the descendants and successors of these overland immigrants as quite adventurous enough for anybody.

The party left the railroad at its western terminus, Terre Haute, Indiana, and proceeded westward on horseback into Illinois, where, in the region of Pulaski, Chile, Columbus, and Warsaw, the herd of sheep and other live-stock was brought together, ferried across the Mississippi at Keokuk, Iowa, and thence started on the long overland journey. The route appears to have been the usual one taken by westward-bound emigrants. From Fort Kearney, opposite Council Bluffs, they proceeded up the Platte river, swinging northward towards the base of the Black Hills as they passed out of Nebraska into Wyoming. They found themselves in frequent contact with Mormon trains on their way to Salt Lake. Not the least interesting portion of the diary are the references to the Mormons and to their famous leader, Brigham Young. It appears that many of the overland travellers found the Saints rather difficult to deal with, though our diarist is obliged to confess to fair and courteous treatment.

To students of recent California history, the Diary will have names and incidents of considerable interest. Col. W. Hollister, after whom the town of Hollister California, was named, brought

iv

his flock of sheep on the same route, sometimes passing and sometimes following, the Flint-Bixby party. The Burdick referred to is almost certainly 'Judge 'Cyrus Burdick, later a prominent citizen of San Gabriel and Los Angeles. Long Beach, California was built upon the holdings of Llewellyn Bixby and other members of the Bixby family. The building up of the livestock industry of California was the result of precisely such adventures as herein set forth.

The present Diary came to the writer's attention through Mrs. Sarah Bixby Smith, daughter of the Llewellyn Bixby above mentioned. Readers of this Diary may be interested to know that Mrs. Smith is about to publish a volume of memoirs[3] dealing with the early American period in Southern California, and based in part on this Diary, which will thus become a piece justificative to accompany her account. Mrs. Smith has assisted in editing the Diary. A valuable feature of the above mentioned volume will be an account of the later history of the Flint-Bixby firm.

The sketch map that accompanies this Diary is intended as a general guide for the reader; no claim to technical accuracy is made for it.

WALDEMAR WESTERGAARD.

Claremont, California,1924

---

[3] See *Adobe Days* by Sarah Bixby Smith. First published in 1925 and more recently by University of Nebraska Press in its Bison Books imprint.

1851-1853 – California and Back

May 21st, 1851:

Left my childhood home for California, in company with Cousins Lewellyn[4] and Amasa Bixby of Norridgewock.

Arrived in New York by rail from Boston evening of 22nd, stopping at the Judson Hotel.

May 28th:

Sailed from New York on steamship Crescent City Capt. Taney for Chagres. Found on ship 45 other passengers from the state of Maine.

Had all the inconveniences of a crowded ship with the resulting growling, rowing, an occasional personal combat between the crew and passengers. We spent most of the time night and day on deck, the fresh air being less conducive to sea sickness than the close contaminated atmosphere below.

June 6th:

Arrived at the Bay of Chagres, mouth of Chagres River. Was taken off steamship in small boats handled by natives of the small

---

[4] Llewellyn Bixby was the third son of Amasa Bixby and Fanny Weston Bixby, and was born in Norridgewock, Maine, on October 4, 1825. He died in Los Angeles, California, on December 5, 1896. He was a first cousin of Thomas and Benjamin Flint, and all three were grandchildren of Benjamin Weston and Anna Powers Weston of Madison, Maine. [1923]

village of thatched huts of the native population and board shanties of the adventurous white skinned race.

We passed on the left going in the old Spanish Fort an insignificant defence when compared with later built fortifications.

Left Chagres at 2 o'clock. Started up river on a small stern wheel steamboat owned and commanded by Capt. Jewett[5], a Maine man from the City of Bangor. Night coming on the boat was made fast to a stump at a place called "Dos Hermanos"—a landing point near the line of the Panama Railroad where men were working in the swamp bordering the river. Found a man from Indiana there keeping what was called the U. S. Hotel who was quite sick with an attack of Cholera Morbus. Stayed with him some four hours, gave him some medicine much to his relief. Charged him $15.00 and returned to the decks of the steamboat to camp down for the night. Room on the decks was scarcely obtainable, having been all preempted before my return; by crowding some of my friends managed to get a recumbent position and so passed the night. Learned that a man from South Boston had fallen overboard and not seen again after striking the turbid river waters made so by recent heavy rains.

June 7th:

Early in the morning our boat was started up river again for its destination Gorgona but at noon Capt. Jewett landed and ordered

---

[5] An A. J. Jewett is reported to have arrive in Panama "early in the month of December [1850], with the frames, machinery, and every thing requisite for the construction of two steamers, which were to be placed on the Chagres River. Mr. J, thought he would have the steamboats put up, and every thing in running order, in the course of fifty days, so that it is quite likely they are now ready for the trade. This is a desideratum long and anxiously wished for, and one which cannot fail of producing a rich harvest for the enterprising projector." Sacramento Transcript February 27, 1851.

all the passengers into small native boats to be taken through in them. As the steamer was much more comfortable and the scenery could be much better enjoyed from it, we naturally were much opposed to the change and harsh language was used on both sides. Matters looked a little warlike when Gen. Hitchcock took a hand so effectually as to convince Capt. Jewett that he had better carry out his agreement with the passengers and all was serene again. General H. was on his way to California to take command of the Pacific Division of the U. S. Army[6]. Capt. Jewett wished to get his passengers off the boat so he could return to Chagres for another lot of passengers expected next day by steamship Orizaba. Arrived at Gorgona that evening. Most of the passengers going ashore, by permission of Capt. Jewett we spread our blankets again on the deck of his boat for the night. The heavy tropical vegetation upon the river banks was a novelty to those of us who for the first time had an opportunity to observe it. The naked native children and lightly clad elderly ones filled in an occasional picture.

June 8th:

Breakfasted at an American Hotel of which there were three at that time in Gorgona after which we took passage in a boat which was propelled by six natives with long poles —twelve passengers to a boat. The natives were strong, muscular fellows, perfectly made — whenever they got heated in working through rapids, they would dash themselves with water using large gourds. In places they had to get into the water and push the boat against the current. Arrived at Cruces at noon. Dined at Dinsmore—hired our baggage packed on mules for Panama and started on foot to cross the dividing ridge between Atlantic and Pacific oceans. Arrived at

---

[6] Brevet Brigadier General Ethan A. Hitchcock held that command 1851–1853.

Frenches Halfway House about dark. Were fortunate in finding cots and a pair of blankets each for the night. Was disturbed in our slumbers by those of our fellow travelers who waited to obtain mules for the ride across, about 11 o'clock, and there were not cots or blankets for them.

June 9th:

Started early in the morning—tramping along leisurely — bathing now and then in the pure mountain pools—and arrived a little after dark in Panama. Knowing we would have to wait several days for the steamship Northerner for which we had tickets we engaged board in the Western Hotel kept by a man named Allen from Lowell, Mass, at $10 per week. Panama at this time was quite free from sickness and we spent the time very pleasantly in and around the old walled city.

June 15th:

Went on board steamship Northerner, Capt. Randall and sailed for San Francisco next day (16th). We found ourselves on another ship crowded to its utmost limits and the food question, an all absorbing one. I luckily found an opportunity to make the acquaintance of the baker which I improved to the extent of getting a pie now and then and some hot rolls with butter occasionally. We were deck passengers and slept under an awning over the quarter deck in Standee berths, when we could get them, some large stuffed chairs laid down made me a pretty good substitute for pillow and I got accustomed to sleeping on the deck floor so would not trouble myself to hunt for anything softer even after arriving in California.

We soon found ourselves infested with vermin and later observed that all the passengers were addicted to rubbing and scratching. There was no escape so we settled down to a daily slaughter of the rapidly increasing pests.

June 24th:

We arrived at Acapulco where we remained two and a half days.
There we enjoyed the fruits and found somewhat better food in the hotels. Went out into the country for a day's walk on the banks of the Rio Grande where we found a great number of women washing clothes standing in the water and using the rocks for wash boards. They seemed to be washing all their clothes for they did not have a stitch upon their bodies. The idea of being immodest did not seem to impress them in the least, in fact only a little removed from bathers at our fashionable sea side resorts.

Returning from our walk as we got into town we saw a crowd of excited Mexicans rushing through the streets— heard some shots and soon learned that a returning Californian had been killed, shot by a posse of city police. The shooting naturally created considerable excitement among the Americans or rather Anglo-Americans who at that time numbered some 2,500—three passenger steamships being in port. Inquiry developed that he was a rough character from California named Brekenridge and had caused no little difficulty among the passengers. The verdict "served him right" for having used his pistol when the attempt to arrest him was made by the police—shooting a native in the knee and luckily for the crowd his other three shots did not strike any one.

The Northerner having taken in coal and water for balance of voyage sailed on eve of 26th. Off the cape of St. Lucas had a cold norther which induced the passengers to gather into all the warm corners of the ship. The smoke stack was particularly sought for.

July 4th:

Put into outer Bay of San Diego—to land the mails for that place—and took on shipboard two large steers. The band of cattle was driven to the water's edge, the two selected, lassoed, dragged into the water, towed out to the side of the ship and hauled aboard with a rope around the horns—one a large black fellow was slaughtered for the celebration dinner.

Came near running ashore at Point San Pedro. Passengers got up a little celebration. A copy of the Declaration could not be found on the ship so that important part of the usual programme had to be omitted. Met the P. M. S. S. Oregon bound for Panama gaily decked out with flags.

July 6th:

Ran into the Bay of Monterey and sent mails ashore in a boat for that old capital.

July 7th:

(47 days from Anson. 40 days from N. Y. 22 days from Panama.)

Arrived in San Francisco. Landed in small boat on Clay Street, near Montgomery. The debris from the recent May[7] fire driven about by the strong trade wind made the city decidedly uncomfortable—and we were glad to get aboard the steamer Hartford at 4 o'clock P. M. for Sacramento where we arrived early on the morning of the 8th. Found accommodations at the "Lady Adams" hotel—where we got rid of the pests of the Northerner.

July 10th:

---

[7] May 3rd-May 4th, 1851. The major portion of the city was destroyed.

Started from Sacramento for Volcano Diggings (Amador County) with a freight wagon—having the privilege of riding on level and downhill. Camped that night on the Macosme (Cosumne) River. Preferred lodgings on a hay stack rather than contend with fleas indoors.

July 11th:

Camped again at Amador, had same kind accommodations as the previous night.

July 12th:

Arrived about noon in Volcano the objective point when we started from Maine 53 days out. At which place I met my brother Benjamin who had preceeded me, having left Anson in February, 1849 and arrived in San Francisco on the ship Humboldt from Panama in August of that year.

The Diary of Dr. Thomas Flint

1852 - 1853 Back to Maine

1852—Saturday, Christmas Day, 25th December:

Left Volcano on a round trip journey from California to Maine and back again to California "across the plains." Brother Benjamin[8], Cousin Lewellyn Bixby and myself having agreed to unite our fortunes for the undertaking of bringing to California sheep and cattle, more for the trip than profit.

Ben and Lewell went to the Buena Vista Ranch to settle accounts with Messrs. Stone and Baker and I took passage on a freight wagon for Sacramento.

December 27th:

The morning was bright and pleasant. The ground covered a foot or more deep with snow from a heavy storm a few days previous which flooded the country, rendering the roads nearly impassible. We had to pick our way as best we could. The four mules were often mired down and had to be gotten out one at a time. In two days we made Sacramento, about 45 miles. The city mostly under water and but partly rebuilt from a destructive fire in July.

Ben and Lewell met me there, having had fully as rough time getting there as I had.

8

Benjamin was the second son of William R. and Electa W. Flint, and was born in New Vineyard, Maine, on February 27, 1827. He died at Sant Juan Buatista, California, October 3, 1881 [1923]

December 28th:

Started for San Francisco. Our hack from hotel to steamboat was a flat-bottom boat drawn by a horse through the mud, sometimes afloat with water well up the sides of the horse. Took River Steamer Confidence. No trouble in running a steamboat for the Sacramento River was 12 miles wide.

December 29th to 31st:

In San Francisco prospecting for a passage to New York—by steamship, 1st cabin $300, and get across the Isthmus from Panama at your own expense. Express charges on gold to New York high.

After much time spent at transportation offices we finally concluded on taking a steerage passage on the steamship Northerner, Capt. Isham, for Panama—as we found the ship had been completely overhauled and what was the 2nd cabin newly fitted up for 3rd class passengers and it was her first trip after the change. Besides there were very few passengers. Fare to Panama $50, in opposition to Mail Line.

1853—January 1st:

Concluded to carry our gold on our persons stowed in buckskin jackets made for the purpose. Sailed in the morning. Soon found the gold, some $3,500 each, burdensome. Could not get it any way so it would not drag and become painful night or day. We therefore took possession of a berth, there being plenty of them and put our jackets between two mattresses and made ourselves comfortable. One of us sleeping over our deposit nights and being on guard during the day.

January 8th:

Celebrated the anniversary of the battle of New Orleans by a sunset gun. In the evening had songs and address by Col.-, etc.

January 9th:

In Acapulco again. Ben and I went ashore. Lewell stayed by our deposit. An earthquake had shaken up things badly since our visit in June, '51. At 8 o'clock P. M. sailed on our course again for Panama.

January 13th:

Head winds. Ocean very rough. Seasick. Passengers execrating a sea voyage. Old Neptune treated with most uncomplimentary language.

January 14th:

Sea calmed down. First land seen since crossing the Gulf of Tehuantepec. Passengers become jovial and joking remarks are in order.

January 15th:

Coasting along towards the Bay of Panama during the day which we entered through a narrow passage just at dark.

January 16th:

Steaming along in Bay of Panama for the city. Arrived early in the morning. Were advised to spend but little time in the city on account of the hostility of the natives from a recent riot with passengers. Before leaving the steamship we packed our gold in a small chest we had for our blankets and clothing. It was so large that the weight was not sufficient to rouse curiosity or suggest its contents. A small valise or satchel having gold in it would be snatched or stolen if not closely watched and backed with a revolver.

January 17th:

Landed from the anchorage in small boats early in the morning—contracted with a native muleteer to pack our chest across to Cruces on the Chagres River. We kept the mule with our valuable cargo in sight most of the time. About sunset arrived at the Halfway station. Near the summit of the divide between the waters of the Pacific and Atlantic we took possession of a vacant hut, built a fire in the center and started to get supper when there came in quite a large party of passengers for California, a number of women and children from New Orleans they said. It had been raining, they were drenching wet—their mules had acted badly and bucked them off and they had to wade and wallow through muddy pools, their thin shoes were poor protection to their feet. All in all they were in a most abject and dilapidated condition. The hut could not accommodate all so we asked our guide how far it was to another stopping place where we could get something to eat. He said it was one league, so we repacked, left our good fire and started out knowing it would be dark before we could get through, so it was and the longest one league ever experienced. Getting to our objective place we tried to rouse some one but no response but our guide knew how to get into the hut, which we entered but found no provisions of any sort. We got out our dry clothes and blankets and prepared to rest as comfortably as possible. There were several bunks and a scaffolding over one end so we managed to find places to lie down.

About 11 o'clock the owner of the place came home and proceeded to prepare his supper of rice with a little dried meat boiled together but from the size of the pot it was evident he was not keeping a restaurant. About the time the stew was done we slung a little Spanish lingo at him and so got pretty familiar with the result that we three got a pint cup each of the rice and meat which satisfied our hunger completely—but not another fellow got a taste.

As good luck would have it a native came in with a good sized bag of bakers bread which he parted with seemingly very reluctantly at a large profit and the other fellows appetites were appeased—all told there were 14 of us.

January 18th:

Arrived at Cruces about 10 o'clock in the morning and first move was to get something to eat. Contracted for a chicken and eggs meal, were told it would be ready in an hour. In the meantime we engaged a boat to take us down the Chagres River to Barbacoa to which place the Panama Railroad had been completed.

We were summoned by a bell to our breakfast, started on coffee, bread and eggs, but no chicken. There were five of us. As the contract called for chicken we made the demand. Our boatman was anxious to get away of course, but we did not budge, thinking there might be some collusion. The chicken finally was produced but it was so tough we had to give up and paid our 75c and started down the river for the railroad terminus. Found the little river steamboat in which we came up to same place in '51 used for a restaurant in which we took our next meal.

Just at time for the train to start we had a little excitement caused by a Virginian who had induced a negro slave to return to that State with him, but when the negro found friends with the darkies at the station that he was going back to unavoidable slavery again and could escape by stopping there where he could not be legally held he accepted the situation and did not respond when called by his owner, whereat the owner asked that the train be held a few minutes. His friends with much bragadocio swore they would get the d—d n— anyhow, so started to get him, knowing he was up in a garret nearby. They made a rush for the garret and started to ascend a rickety stairway when they were told to stop and looking up saw a lot of big bore Mexican muskets (Escopatas) pointed close to their heads. They naturally did not want the n— so bad as they did a few minutes before, and crestfallen came aboard the train. We who were not in sympathy enjoyed the outcome.

Many slave owners brought negroes with them to California to dig gold for them.

Reached Aspinwall by rail and found an independent steamship about to sail for New York on which we engaged passage in an upper deck cabin for $25.00 each, making $75.00 from San Francisco to New York.

Put into Kingston Jamaica for coal. Lewell stayed by our deposit on the steamship—though it was in a large trunk or chest. Ben and I went ashore for a few hours.

1853—January 27th:

Arrived in New York early in the morning. Left our baggage in a hotel on Fulton Street. Took our gold in a valise and started for Philadelphia by Camden and Amboy railroad. Arrived at Washington Hotel, Philadelphia, about 9 o'clock that evening. Took a room together for safety as the negro porter's eyes looked wild when packing in our valise—it weighed over 50 pounds. The next day took the gold to the U. S. Mint. Had to wait a day for it to be assayed, everything in shape of gold had to pass through the assayer's department, $50 slugs—coin from private mints of San Francisco and native gold.

January 29th:

Got our mint receipt of the value of our deposit. We were dressed a little rough when we arrived in Philadelphia and at the hotel were seated at the most inconvenient table, but as we dressed up somewhat and the report of our gold got more and more known we got pretty well up in the dining room before we left the Washington. I had boarded there for a time in 1848.

Left for New York and arrived there in the evening. January 30th:

Started on morning train for Boston, arrived there about 8 or 9 o'clock, went to the U. S. Hotel. House full so we were cotted in one of the parlors where there was a good fire which we enjoyed to perfection as it was clear, cold weather, a great change from the tropical climate of Aspinwall and Jamaica.

January 31st:

Started for Maine in the morning by railroad to Waterville where we arrived—the end of the road[9]—about 6 o'clock that evening. Coldest of cold weather. Got supper at the Elmwood. Met a few acquaintances who made us talk of California, and as the stage for North Anson left at 7 o'clock, took it for an 18 mile ride. It was so cold we had curtains drawn and buttoned down tight, stopped at Norridgewock to leave mail and warm up. Left Mr. Bixby at his father's door and got to our old home about 11 o'clock. One solid month from San Francisco.

---

[9] Perhaps referring to the termination of the Androscoggin & Kennebec Railroad's tracks.

February 1st:

At first glance out of my window was surprised in my recollection of the landscape before me. What was large and high to me when a child seemed dwarfed. The fields did not appear to be more than garden patches in California. The country was comparatively level. Mountains Saddleback, Abraham and Bigelow were but hills and nearby. The Kennebec River was diminished to a small stream. Yet it was all beautiful in a mantle of purest snow—and in a short time my mind balanced the difference between the broad valleys and high mountains of California, and I was at home again.

From February 1st to March 8th:

At father's home in North Anson most of the time. Went to Farmington to visit my aged grandfather Dr. Thos. Flint then 86 years old. We had visitors by score almost daily who came to ask if we had seen their friends who had gone to California. All seemed to be impressed with the idea that we must know everybody in the State. At least might have seen their friends. We were among the few that had returned from the far distant land of gold, therefore were objects of interest. We talked until our vocal organs could stand the strain no longer and were glad to start west on March 8th:

1853 - Across Country to California

Tuesday [March] 8th:

Left father's[10] house by stage for Waterville. At uncle Amasa Bixby's Lewell joined us and the overland party was united again, viz., brother Benjamin, Cousin Lewellyn Bixby and myself. City of Portland was our stopping place for the night. Ben and I had our deguerotypes taken. Met Hon. David Bronson[11], Gen. Frank Smith, wife and daughter Emma and cousin Thomas H. Weston—stopped at U. S. Hotel.

Wednesday 9th:

Started for Boston on 8 o'clock A. M. train, Ben and Lewell remaining until the afternoon train. Reached Boston about 2 o'clock; at Elm House. Exchanged our money at Suffolk Bank for their bills as they were good anywhere West and none other were. Ben and Lewell arrived in the evening.

Thursday 10th:

---

[10] William Reed Flint (1796 - 1887), North Anson, Maine. Among other interests he was involved in the woolen trade and, in parallel with his son across the country in California, was involved the introduction of fine blooded stock of Spanish Merinos--especially from Vermont when that state had the lead in fine wooled sheep. See the afterward for mention of Thomas Flint's involvement in the wool business. See https://www.wikitree.com/wiki/Flint-3176

[11] David Bronson, 1800-1863; a lawyer who began his practice in North Anson, Maine, near the Flint homestead. A former member of Congress, elected to the 27th congress fulfill the vacancy caused by the resignation of George Evans.

8 o'clock A. M. on the Western R. R. for Albany. Saw Henry Watson at Springfield, Mass. A freshet had washed away the approaches to R. R. Bridge at Albany, so were taken across the Hudson River by ferry boat. Made the Delavan House our stopping place in Albany. Pleasant weather. Saw the city by gas light.

Friday 11th:

8 o'clock A. M. off for Buffalo. Found Capt. Rounds in the cars. Got to Buffalo at 11 o'clock P. M. Put up at the Clarendon House. Tired. Stormy. Had a facetious Englishman along according to his own estimate of himself.

Saturday 12th:

Took a stroll about Buffalo and left for Cincinnati at 11 o'clock A. M. via Cleveland and Columbus. Arrived in Cleveland at 8 o'clock P. M. Columbus next where we changed cars.

Sunday 13th:

4 o'clock A. M. in Columbus. Arrived in Cincinnati at 10 1/2 o'clock A. M. Went to the Gibson House. Met Dr. J. F. Noyes[12] who was expecting us there. Tired from an all night ride. (No sleeping cars at that time.)[13] 1,107 miles from North Anson.

Monday 14th:

---

[12] Dr J. F. Noyes had practiced in Waterville, and had observed the autopsy of the murder victim discussed in the first introduction. Flint had sutured the incisions on the body after the initial autopsy was completed. Noyes eventually returned to Waterville.

[13] Later interpolation made by Dr. Flint. [1923]

Rested in Cincinnati.

Tuesday 15th:

In the P. M. went out to Dayton by railroad so as to start by early train for Indianapolis and Terre Haut. Stopped at the Phillips House.

Wednesday 16th:

Called at 2 o'clock A. M., went aboard cars at 2 1/2. No breakfast, nor could we get a mouthful until we arrived in Indianapolis at 2 1/2 o'clock P. M. The R. R. was new, rough, and no stations by the way. Arrived in Terre Haut about 5 o'clock. The end of railroad on the west. The balance of the trip to the Pacific must be made by horseback or afoot. Stopped at the Prairie House.

Thursday 17th:

In Terre Haut. Preparing for the journey across Illinois. Light rain.

Friday 18th:

Bought three horses and fitted saddles to them. Wrote letters, etc. Pleasant.

Saturday 19th:

Left for Paris, 22 miles across river in Illinois. Pleasant weather. Roads as bad as mud can make them. Arrived about sunset.

Sunday 20th:

In Paris. Attended the Presbyterian church in the morning. Hymns lined and the Chorister led the singing, making the most ludicrous grimaces.

In the afternoon rode out 10 miles to Bloomfield. Found a hotel with good beds. Still pleasant.

Monday 21st:

Rode out to Ridge Farm. Called at George W. Hayworths to see an acquaintance sister Ann made when she was in that section. From there went to Quaker Point, Indiana to see cousins that were Sophia and Abigail Mace. A roundabout, crooked way to get there but Ben and I had a pleasant visit. 18 mile ride. Pleasant.

Tuesday 22nd:

Took dinner with friend G. W. Hayworth. From there went to Georgetown. Stopped at the Dunseth House where we found Lewell who went ahead yesterday. 13 mile ride. 15 miles from Bloomfield.

[Wednesday] 23rd:

Called in forenoon upon G. W. Holloway. Wrote a letter to Ann. Got two horses shod. Clothed Lewell in a rubber suit as he could not stand the chilly weather on account of fever from change of climate. Put off across the prairie for Sidney, 28 miles, where we arrived about sunset. Cold, bleak, windy ride. Geese, ducks, prairie chickens seen in abundance.

[Thursday] 24th:

Called early after a good night's rest. Lewell troubled with toothache after being filled. Dined at Urbana. Bixby had his tooth "hauled." Shiretown of Champagne County. Arrived at Middletown House for the night. 24 miles ride for the day. Six beds in a 7x9 room. Fried eggs floating in lard, almost the universal food in this part of the world. Pleasant weather.

Friday 25th:

Left in good time. Dined at Mt. Pleasant. Cold, raw, windy weather. Arrived at Leroy at sunset. Roads across the prairie. Muddy of worst kind. 25 miles. Clear at sunset.

Saturday 26th:

Rode from Leroy to Bloomington, the county seat of McLean County, where we dined in company with a Pennsylvania cattle dealer who gave us his ideas of business. Could not get to put up in Lexington but were fortunate in getting an invitation to spend the night at a private house in Twin Grove, the best we have found in Illinois.

[Sunday] 27th:

Went to Peoria through timber land of poor quality. Dined at Moreton. Put up at the Clinton House. 52 miles from Leroy. Draw in bridge broken so crossed the Illinois River in a boat.

Monday 28th:

Left Peoria. Dined at Trivoli, Fulton County. Spent the night at McCutchins where Bixby and I went to look at his sheep. Price

$8.50 per head. Ben and Dan, a helper, went on another route. 36 miles for the day's ride.

Tuesday 29th:

Dined at Canton. Joined Ben and Dan. Left after dining and at 5 o'clock were in Cuba. A small place 12 miles from Canton through a good country. Looks quite Yankee like. Sent a letter to father.

Wednesday 30th:

Put off for Bernadotti through a poor section. Arrived at 11 o'clock—a small village on Goose Creek. Stopped for the night in Vermont, a pretty village in Fulton County. We stopped at Mr. Dumross' Hotel (Ben, Bixby, Dan and I). A warm day. Distance called 21 miles from Cuba. We found that when told that a place was a *quarter* away, that it might be a mile and a half, three sides of a quarter section of land, a quarter section being half a mile square.

Thursday 31st:

Beds last night good, but most miserably made up, could scarcely sleep in them. Breakfast decidedly poor. Flapjacks and molasses, the only eatable substance. Dined in Broklyn, a small village. Started for Augusta but missed the road and got Pulaski. Put up at a Methodist tavern. Rather unpleasant on account of a sick child. Distance today, 40 miles.

April 1st:

Started in good season for Quincy via Columbus. Dined in Columbus and got to Quincy about 8 o'clock in the evening. Had a hard time finding the town. Most of the way through oak wooded prairie, uncultivated. Registered at the Quincy House. Horses and ourselves well tired out. Pleasant. Distance 38 miles.

Saturday 2nd:

Spent in Quincy—getting all the information we could in regard to the surrounding country—sheep and cattle interests, etc. Found James Brown, whose wife was a sister of Mrs. Woods, who with her husband was employed on the Buena Vista Ranch near lone, California, where our headquarters were when in California. Ben and I dined with them. Many invitations to call from those having friends in California. Rainy. Distance traveled horseback from Terre Haut, 348 miles.

Sunday 3rd:

In Quincy. Ben and I passed the evening with the Brown family. Had best apples since leaving Maine. Four children in family. Rainy since Saturday P. M.

[Monday] 4th:

Started East for sheep in the surrounding country. Dined at Ursa. The first whisky hole we have struck for a long time. Passed through Mendon, a pleasant village, and Milford to Houston. Got to stop at a Mr. Thomas. Distance 28 miles.

[Tuesday] 5th:

On the hunt for sheep. Ran into an election. From inquiries began to think we were in poor luck. Sheep were scarce. Dined at Chili. Pleasant hotel with the piazza for a sitting room. Distance 15 miles from Houston.

[Wednesday] 6th:

Dined at Mendon—back to Quincy 30 miles—stopped at Mr. Browns.

[Thursday] 7th:

After dinner started for Chili. Stopped over night at Mendon. Met Dan there whom I had left at Chili to watch for Ben and Lewell. Hard sleeping chance—not straw enough on bed cords.

April 8th:

Dined at Chili. Went to Augusta, 40 miles from Quincy. Good hotel kept by Mr. Curtis—claiming to be a Yankee from N. Y.

Saturday 9th:

Put off for Columbus where we expect to meet Ben and Lewell. Bought 50 sheep south of Pulaski. Dined with Clem Robbins. Stopped near Garretts Mills at Farlows.

Sunday 10th:

Started at sunrise for Columbus 6 miles away. Breakfasted. Found the boys had driven out 6 miles with 400 sheep. Went out to see them. Met Lewell coming in, but I went on to see Ben who had sprained a foot. Returned to town. Got supper and went to bed early.

Monday 11th:

Went from Columbus to Mr. Hulands in the Township of Northeast. A Carolinian by birth.

[Tuesday] 12th:

Put up at Mr. Burks, a Virginian, after a hard jaunt through scrubby oak barrens.

[Wednesday] 13th:

Took dinner with Benjamin Gould, Esq., a Connecticut Yankee who asked me if I had ever peddled any—so I inferred that had been his *profession*. Went on and stopped with Nathan Robbins— a Carolinian by descent and a hunter.

[Thursday] 14th:

Dined with Clem Robbins and came back to Nathan's to pass the night again. 9 sheep ran away and it took up until 11 o'clock to get them back. At 12 o'clock *started* across the prairie for Chili with 151 sheep and 35 lambs. Arrived at sunset. Put up at the Chili Hotel.

[Friday] 15th:

At one o'clock went back to the sheep and drove them 13 miles to Chili. Also brought along a yoke of oxen. Hard driving the latter part of the drive.

[Saturday] 16th:

Went from Chili to meet Ben at Houston. Found him at Mrs. Newlands. Lewell came in just at dark. So we were together again.

Sunday 17th:

Spent the day at Mrs. Newlands a widow with two daughters and a son. Fashion of the country for belles and beaux to get together Sunday nights. The son was away so when we returned, not being in the courting line of business and occupying the room with the one the young man would return to, some time towards morning we set the chairs against the door so when he came in there was a grand racket much to his chagrin when called upon to explain at the breakfast table.

Monday 18th:

Left for the vicinity of Garretts Mills and Lewell for the Clayton neighborhood. Ranged the country with J. R. Harrington in a rain and at night brought up at William Lewises, a Kentuckian.

April 19th:

Met Lewell at Mr. Gores where we dined. In afternoon drove to Eben C. Downings for the night. Small house, and the bed given us was foot to foot with the family bed where a brat of a youngster kept us awake until after midnight yelling to have the candle lighted, which the mother did not care to do. Ben started for Quincy by way of Bloomfield.

[Wednesday] 20th:

Started for Chili feeling pretty well used up for want of sleep. Got through in good time. Found we had got together 1,034 sheep and six yoke of oxen.

[Thursday] 21st:

From Chili started for Warsaw herding sheep along over the prairie but in severe thunder storm. Used my saddle for an umbrella. Reached a place marked on the map in large letters, St. Albans. Made inquiry for the town and was shown a lot of stakes for the corners of a lot of lots. One pretty fair house but could not be accommodated for the night but got shelter in a small hut already well filled with a family but it was on the extension principle for two sets of trundle beds were drawn out from under the big one whilst we were stowed away in a corner left —cooking utensils and tin dishes decidedly short, however fried eggs, bacon and corn bread were at our disposal, with saxafras tea for breakfast.

April 22nd:

Drove along slowly for the sheep to feed for the forenoon. Left the flock in charge of Bixby and help and went to Warsaw to make arrangements for a place to shear the sheep and shearers to do it. Put up at the Warsaw Hotel. Ben joined me there.

Saturday 23rd:

Stormy in the morning. About noon went out to meet the flock and drive them into Dr. English's pasture 3 miles from town. Returned to Warsaw to take boat for Quincy. Found had to wait until morning.

Sunday 24th:

Half past six o'clock. Took the steam packet Kate Kearny for Quincy. Got down at noon. Dined at the Quincy House. Cleaned up. Went to church with the Browns. Rainy in P. M.

Monday 25th:

Woke up with the sun shining full into the room. Completely rested. Nearly a cloudless morning in contrast with a gloomy night. Bought 2 wagons at $163.00; 14 blankets at $52.75. Evening at Browns. To bed early.

Tuesday 26th:

Left Quincy for Bloomfield. Dined at Henry Kemps. After dinner started 131 sheep for Warsaw. Stopped for the night at a Mr. Turner's, an old man 80 years old living with son. From Livermore, Maine. 18 years in Illinois. The young man married a Connecticut woman. Good building, wood pile and surroundings generally indicated a genuine Yankee.

[Wednesday] 27th:

Bloomfield prairie mostly settled by immigrants from the State of Maine. Found a Stevens family from Norridgewock. A beautiful section of country. Drove to Lima, a poverty [stricken] and shiftless looking place.

[Thursday] 28th:

Awakened by flashes of lightning and rattling of thunder to look out upon severe storm which lasted all day, so did not start out, for the streams were bank full. Guarded the sheep on the public square.

Friday 29th:

Called up last night by the illness of Mr. Harry S. Kemp who was helping us drive. Got some remedies for his cold from the landlord. He is unable to help today. The rest of us drove to Warsaw where we found Ben and Lewell engaged in shearing sheep.

Saturday 30th:

Took care of the sheared sheep out on the prairie. Something like work for the sheep were not accustomed to being held in that manner but the ground was quite dry so it was good riding.

Sunday, May 1st:

With Daniel Hendrickson took care of sheep again- boarding with Moses Hammond, a Massachusetts man, and family. Rainy in the P. M.

Monday 2nd:

Herded sheep again alone, taking my dinner in my pocket. Rainy in the A. M. Mr. Gilliam a California acquaintance sent $1,000.00 by Hankerson to Lewell.

Tuesday 3rd:

On the prairie again with sheep assisted by Salem Hammond, a boy. Getting to be quite a large flock making considerable work to keep them together as they naturally break up into small lots.

Wednesday 4th:

Out with the sheep again with Dan. Wet and uncomfortable. Ground so soft it is hard getting around on our horses.

Thursday 5th:

Still a shepherd with a dog, the first day I have had one. Should have a gun for the wolves are troublesome, not so much so on the prairie as near timber.

Friday 6th:

Finished shearing. Am at leisure except to look out that the men keep the sheep together.

Saturday 7th:

Started off for the overland journey with 1,880 sheep, young and old. 11 yoke of oxen, 2 cows, 4 horses, 2 wagons, complete camping outfit, 4 men, 3 dogs and ourselves. Crossed Mississippi River at Keokuk by ferry, $62. Now in Iowa.

Sunday 8th:

In Keokuk. Visited the Mormon Camp where it was said there were 3,400 proselytes from Europe. 278 emigrant wagons ready to convey them to Salt Lake. A motley crowd of English, Welsh, Danes, etc. Took in a part of their religious ceremonies.

Monday 9th:

Helped start out the train for Council Bluffs across Iowa. Returned to Warsaw myself to look for a sale of the wool.

Tuesday 10th:

Packing wool.

Wednesday 11th:

Finished packing wool. Sold it to Connable Smith & Co. at 24 1/2c per lb., delivered at their store in Keokuk.

Thursday 12th:

Hired help and hauled wool to landing to be shipped to Keokuk. Cold day. Tired.

Friday 13th:

My birthday, 29 years old. A beautiful, clear day. Wandered upon the bank of the Father of Waters, waiting for steamer to ship to Keokuk. The De Vernon came up the river in the afternoon so I shipped myself and wool for Keokuk.

Saturday 14th:

Weighed and delivered 6,410 lbs. to Connable Smith & Co., amounting to $1,570.45. The banker at Keokuk asked me to take in payment for my check English sovereigns at 1c more than actual value as they would pass for $5.00 in all places west of Missouri

River. I could afford and would afford to speculate. The steamer I was to take was whistling "All aboard" and in his hurry he passed me ten pieces too much and I thought so at the time but could not stop, so put the money in a pocket by itself, jumped aboard steamboat for Quincy. On steamer Lamartine. Counted money and found mistake. Expected to hear from the banker as he knew where I would stop in Saint Louis, so waited. Arrived in Quincy and stopped at the Browns.

Sunday 15th:

Attended three church sermons at Congregational church. That would have to last me through to California.

Monday 16th:

Left Quincy by steamer for Saint Louis. Arrived at 9 1/2 o'clock P. M. Had to cross the decks of five steamers to get off. Registered at the Monroe Hotel.

Tuesday 17th:

The agent of the Keokuk banker found me, showed his figures whereby he made the mistake and I paid him his money. "No mistakes rectified after leaving the counter" was pasted conspicuously in his bank.

Weather getting uncomfortably warm.

Wednesday 18th:

Hot as blazes in city.

Thursday 19th:

Still in Saint Louis. In the evening went to Wymans Hall and heard Prof. Agassiz lecture on Geology. Evening comfortable. Not much beauty in the female part of the audience.

Friday 20th:

St. Louis. Mailed letter to father. Comfortable weather.
Purchased a general outfit for the plains from ox yokes to tobacco. Some extra pounds of tea, sugar and coffee to trade with the Mormons or roadside dealers.

Saturday 21st:

3 o'clock on board steamboat El Paso for Council Bluffs, my outfit having been shipped beforehand. Sailed at 6 o'clock up the Missouri. 4 lady passengers upper deck, 2 below, and a U. S. Surveyor going high up the river. The El Paso intended to run up to the Yellowstone. Capt. Tilton and pilot Robinson.

Sunday 22nd:

Air seemed cold. Had 14 Baptist ministers aboard going to a convention at Glasgow, Mo. A Dr. Lynch of Covington, Ky., was particularly opposed to infant baptism. It naturally followed that there was religious services on deck.

Monday 23rd:

At Jefferson City. Cold winds. The management of the boat admirable. No negroes aboard. Officer and crew attentive to the passengers. River rising fast from melting snow in the Rocky Mountains. Prayer meeting at end of saloon. Cards the other.

Tuesday 24th:

Having a bad cold. Some better in P. M. Clergymen left this morning at Glasgow. Pleasant but cold. Running at the rate of 100 miles a day.

Wednesday 25th:

Feeling better of my cold. Patronized the barber at a cost of 10c. Getting along merrily. Met a man who came east with us last winter from California, now living on the river. Kansas City. Took aboard a lot of U. S. mules and oxen.

Thursday 26th:

Indians on the banks at night—at Fort Leavenworth this A. M. Took a walk through the town. Mostly barracks and two old forts. Square lower story stone, upper wood with the corners projecting over the stone midway between stone corners. Making an octagonal facing to all sides. A few soldiers around. 480 miles from St. Louis. At 10 o'clock at a woodyard a wedding party came aboard. Green was the prevailing color with them. After having a jolly greeting they disappeared in the green forest.

Friday 27th:

At St. Joseph early in the morning—a city of 5,000 or 6,000. Sailed at 3 o'clock. Number of passengers increased by parties going to California. Tied up for the night at Savannah Landing. Pleasant evening.

Saturday 28th:

Fine day and beautiful scenery of woods and prairie. Iowas and Shawnee Indians came down to the shore as we passed their villages. The Capt. tossed crackers ashore to them. Laid by on the Nebraska side near an Indian village. The Captain relating Indian and other experiences. River full of sand bars shifting all the time—besides the current was very swift on account of which could not run at night. Storm of hail, thunder and lightning.

Sunday 29th:

Getting above moral and religious influences as we leave civilization behind—and touch the wild and woolly West.
Passed Fort Kearney and mouths of Platt River, saw a lot of Ottoes (Ottowa?) Indians dressed out in all their toggery. Sarpas a kind of an Indian mission.

Monday 30th:

Arrived at the Bluffs.

Tuesday 31st:

Ben came down to the boat to meet me, having left his train a little distance out of Council Bluffs. It took most of the day to get our things off the boat and upon the bank a little back from the river. Covered them with a tent. Supper on crackers and herring. Camped on the goods under the ridge pole.

Wednesday, June 1st:

An uncomfortable night. Thunder, lightning, wind and drizzling rain. Every little while large trees were toppled into the river with a crash, being washed out by the caving of the banks and blown by the wind. The crashing came so frequently that I had to feel my way out to the bank to satisfy myself that I was not near being precipitated with my outfit into the raging Missouri which was rising rapidly from melting snows at its sources. Wrote Dr. Gould— waited impatiently for our teams to report and take away our goods but did not come until well along in the afternoon.

Thursday 2nd:

In Kanesville (Council Bluffs) making preparations for the plains. A town of huts and full of sharp dealers who live off the emigrants by trading, as it is the outpost of the white man for Indians occupy the country across the river.

Friday 3rd:

Went out to assist in bringing in the sheep and cattle. Remained in town with Hendrickson and Jennings, while the others started up the river for the ferry 12 miles above. Helped drive a short distance. Bought another wagon and got what additional supplies we needed. Ripe strawberries on the table.

Saturday 4th:

Started Jennings to overtake train with wagon and ox team. Bought a saddle mare and outfit for $125.00 for my own use. The horse I got in Terre Haute proved a rough one to ride. Lewell came back for some articles not thought of before. Overtook the train at the ferry and camped on the bottom lands near by. Grass excellent.

Sunday 5th:

Wind too strong to attempt crossing the river so had to lay by which is always more troublesome than driving on trail or being busy some way to keep the attention of both men and animals. Horses stampeded in a shower. Ben and Hendrickson after them, returned with them about dark.

Monday 6th:

Commenced ferrying across the Missouri River with one flat boat propelled by oars. 150 head of sheep at a trip. Two other boats were employed ferrying across Mormons. Worked hard all day and only half over. River wide and rapid. Crossed ten loads of sheep. Lewell, Jim and John remained in Nebraska.

Tuesday 7th:

Work at ferrying today. All over but one boat load of horses. Found that the one I had purchased in Kanesville (Council Bluffs) had strayed. Took another and went in pursuit back on the trail, caught it a few miles away, but too late to cross the river, so camped with G. W. Frasher[14], who has 223 head of cattle to ferry over. Paid $57 tolls.

Wednesday 8th:

---

[14] Later in the Diary as Frazer.

Wind blowing a gale. No crossing. Impatient, but no more so than those waiting with their stock to cross. About 700 cattle and 3,500 sheep held up by stress of weather—besides many Mormons.

Thursday 9th:

Assisted Frasher in an attempt to make his cattle swim across the river, but failed. Crossed myself in the boat with the horses. Lewell returned to meet me at the ferry. Took a drink from a spring on West bank of the Missouri and started west over a rolling prairie covered with grass 4 to 6 inches high. Overtook the train and camped near the Elkhorn River.

Friday 10th:

Drove to the ferry and crossed the Elkhorn River. Tolls $41.80. Camped about a mile out on soft bottom land. No high land within several miles. Consider ourselves fairly on the plains. Reports that there are no emigrants nearer than 60 miles ahead. Woeful stories of Indians on the trail ahead. 15 of us in the train. Ben, Lewell, myself, White, Pulman, Jennings, Joe and Dan Hickman, James Force, Henderson, John Trust. Pleasant weather.

Saturday 11th:

Started early. Ben and Lewell have the habit of starting the sheep at 4 o'clock in the morning. We of the last watch start about 6 o'clock. My watch being from 1 to 3 o'clock A. M. Have the whole country in sight to ourselves. Level prairie to sand bluffs on the north. Pleasant weather.

Sunday 12th:

On the trail again. Had to drive 20 miles or more to water. Camped about 1/2 past 6 o'clock, tired. Teaming on though it is Sunday, some of the party not knowing it until mid-day. Less trouble to move on the trail than to care for the stock laying by. Some wolves around but they gave us no trouble. Pleasant.

Monday 13th:

Eleven o'clock A. M. Arrived at Shell creek. Found excellent springs here. Stopped until after dinner. All hands washed up. White had headache, so gave him some compound cathartic pills. Did not drive much today as the sheep are beginning to have sore feet and one yoke of oxen some foot-sore, so drove them singly. Camped. Mosquitoes awful. Pleasant.

Tuesday 14th:

Put off as usual before the last watch started. Ben and Lewell were a long distance ahead. Dan Hendrickson gave chase to a wolf but it proved more than a match for his horse and dog. Extracted a tooth for Hickman. No wood on the route today, nor good water. Camped on the bluff near Loupe Fork. Stormy.

Wednesday 15th:

Today finding we had driven too fast from Elkhorn River concluded not to hurry—found we had accidentally got some 6 miles above the ferry on the Loupe Fork, so had to drive down the river to the crossing. Mosquitoes very troublesome. Five Omaha Indians came into camp and remained until dark. The first aborigine seen. Smoked the Pipe of Peace with them. Tobacco scented with Killikanic. They by signs informed us that they had been unsuccessful on a buffalo hunt and of course a little of something to eat would be acceptable. Pleasant weather.

Thursday 16th:

Ferried our wagons, sheep and horses across the Loupe Fork and swam the cattle. $100.00 paid for ferriage. Camped on the west side. Mosquitoes large and furious. Pleasant.

Friday 17th:

Heavy dew last night. Took a severe cold. Neglected to guard against the dampness sufficiently. Rode part of the day in a wagon. Heat until noon oppressive. Breeze in afternoon. Drove to bluff for camp. No wood near. Travelled about 17 miles. Pleasant.

Saturday 18th:

Feel quite well from effects of a cathartic. Passed 2 graves today, 4 yesterday. The trail this forenoon runs along steep, sandy bluffs on the right for 2 miles—then turns through them to an extensive plain. Horses frightened last night and ran into the sheep, breaking a leg of one which butcher Jennings made mutton of. Sandy bluffs in the west some distance. Pleasant.

Sunday 19th:

Driven out of camp early daylight in the morning by mosquitoes. Drove 7 or 8 miles to an elevation above the general level where there was no blood suckers. Camped for the sabbath and a good rest. The ground had been dug up about there and I picked up the bones of a human foot and other parts of a skeleton which wolves had cleaned of the flesh. Did not report the find for fear some of the boys might feel superstitious about it. Good grass which our animals enjoy, and cannot get out of sight for miles. Pleasant weather.

Monday 20th:

Ben started early with the sheep. Three of our men got tired and homesick. Joe and Dan Hickman being persuaded by Dan Henderson to go back with them. Second watch late in starting. Got along well though short of three men. A big wolf snapped out one of the sheep in the lead. Camped in the bluffs near some ponds. Mosquitoes not bad. Pleasant.

Tuesday 21st:

A hard day's drive brought us to Prairie Creek where we camped. Road a great part of the way in sand hills. Heavy thunder storm about 10 o'clock A. M., after it mosquitoes very aggressive. Considerable game in the ponds, but we got none.

Wednesday 22nd:

Travelled over a level prairie to Wood River, a 15 mile drive. Arriving at 1/2 past 12 o'clock. Crossed on brush bridge similar to the one over Prairie Creek. In the morning George W. Frazer overtook us with his train. Cool and pleasant.

Thursday 23rd:

An Indian undertook to run off Frazer's horses. Same character of country as passed over yesterday. Places accurately described in the Guide Book we have—camped at Prairie Dogtown. Well named. He is a relative of the woodchuck. Pleasant.

Friday 24th:

A steady drive of 12 hours brings us to the two deep ravines opposite to Grand Island. Frazer had a stampede just before camping. His ox teams with the wagons in a wild rush. No damage done but two women in the wagons were somewhat frightened. Pleasant.

Saturday 25th:

A monotonous drive brought to camp between Elm and Buffalo Creeks. Wild cammomile by the way very fragrant. Our stock is getting accustomed to camp life and make the camp their common center, seemingly for sociability and protection. Strong southerly winds all the afternoon and into the night. Some lightning. Our camp three miles above the bridge over Buffalo Creek.

Sunday 26th:

Started early to overtake Ben who got ahead with the sheep. Caught up. Some buffalo came in sight—first seen. Two old bulls came up to the head of the sheep apparently to see us then started for the hills. Ben and I ran them down but could do but little execution with our revolvers. Dined by a good spring on bank of Buffalo Creek where we camped. Pleasant.
Monday 27th:

Camped on Buffalo Creek or a branch of it. Frazer's train close by.
As the moon was coming up at about 1/2 past 12 o'clock in the morning we were suddenly called by the guard crying in alarm, "Ho ho, come here quick", almost at the same instant I heard the click of a flint lock and heavy report of a gun. My pistol, whether

awake or asleep was always at my right hand. The unusual movement of the stock had awakened me for at no time while on the journey did I sleep soundly. Pistol in hand I hurried to where my saddle mare was staked and found James Force dead, two heavy bullets about an ounce each had been shot through from right to left side of the chest which were found one in the blanket— the other just under the skin at point of exit. My mare had been cut loose from her stake-pin but she could not be held as she would drag the strongest man, white or Indian, in the direction of our tent. That was what most likely wakened Force for it was after the time he should have called his relief on duty. The mare was a pointer and would point an Indian, wolf or any wild animal like a dog. So the men or guard used to rest beside her. Though I was immediately at the spot where Force was lying, there was not an Indian in sight—but was most likely in the brush on the bank of the creek.

We hunted the banks somewhat but did not deem it provident to get too close to thick patches of brush nor could we get the dogs to hunt, so we kept guard until daylight. In the morning we dug a grave and having rolled Force in the blanket he was killed in, sorrowfully deposited him in what we would be glad to consider his last resting place, but we well knew the hyenas of the plains would soon dig him out and scatter his bones to the four winds of heaven.

When collecting our stock and some ways from the camp we saw an Indian climbing out on the opposite side of the creek.

We had an Indian appetite and wanted him, so made a rush after him. He was a little too much ahead to be reached by our rifle shots and besides was a fleet runner which may be expected under such circumstances, so that he made the bluffs in safety. About half of our men and of Frazer's were so frightened they hid themselves in such places as seemed to afford protection from Indians.

James Force was an Englishman as he said, about 35 years of age who had inherited quite a fortune and spent it in riotous living, then became a sailor for a time, finally had the California fever and determined to strike the overland trail to work his passage on, and that was the way we picked him up. One day I asked him if he did not think he had made a mistake in spending his money, he said no, for he had had the enjoyment of it and he did not know how much longer he would live.

Two Omaha Indians had been in camp a few days before who carried between them an English musket, old style, with a flint lock and they used for wadding, scraped slippery elm bark dried, such as we found in the wound, hence supposed they had endeavored to steal the horses or a part of them.

Today we saw large herds of buffalos. Some came very near and Lewell shot one for fresh meat, assisted by some of Frazer's men. Camped together (Frazer's and our trains) after a hard shower which cleared off cold. Before 12 o'clock at night we had two stampedes of cattle and horses (sheep never do it), nothing lost however. We surmised Indians were the cause of the stampedes, at any rate the men were terribly wrought up and could see in fancy, Indians behind every bush. No more sleeping on guard.

Tuesday 28th:

William C. Johnson and his wife Mary, left the train they had travelled with thus far and joined ours. Johnson taking one of the ox teams with his wife in the wagon. They were married a short time before leaving Keokuk. Her part of the camp work was to make the bread. No buffalo in sight today. Warm in the middle of the day. Cactus in blossom, yellow in color. After a late drive camped by a small lake. No stampedes as usual of late.

Wednesday 29th:

Struck camp early. Flies in the bluffs very annoying in the morning but did not follow us long. Passed a party of Texas Mormons in camp on Skunk Creek. Soon after we camped. Ben and John caught some fish for supper.

Thursday 30th:

Moved on in good time. Passed the Two Springs, so- called in our guide book 3 1/2 miles out. A foggy and chilly morning. Took our nooning on Mestayer Creek. Afternoon we had showers making the trail muddy in places. Cool all day. Camped on the river a few miles above the forks of the Platt.

July—Friday 1st:

A great deal of alkali water in pools injurious to sheep, lost 3 head on account of drinking it. Crossed numerous creeks and sloughs. A severe tempest about 6 o'clock with hail as large as apples. A stampede of the horses in camp in which one of ours and three of Frazer's ran off but were captured after a good run. Ben, Lewell and I being with the sheep did not get to the camp which was pitched on Bluff Fork by the men with the cattle and horses. Blankets and provisions were brought to us and we stayed with the sheep. No camp fire for the buffalo chips were wet and no wood.

Saturday 2nd:

A hard drive of 15 1/2 miles over hilly and sandy trail but better from yesterday's storm. Camped early on the bank of a small creek. Large white prairie wolves numerous and bold yet it is difficult to get a good shot at them. Pleasant.

Sunday 3rd:

Wolves were troublesome last night but we kept them off so they did not pick up a sheep. Took some shots at them but probably did not hit for if we had the pack would have had a grand howl and killed the wounded one as is their way of doing the wounded up for a meal. Broke camp at 8 o'clock A. M. continuing our way towards the setting sun. If able to compare mosquito-infested places we have passed through, will say that we had today the severest attack for a while, thus far of the whole season. Camped on Rattlesnake Creek. Pleasant.

Monday 4th:

John Palmer from Frazer's camp joined us this morning. Celebrated the day by having an extra supper in which doughnuts of the Yankee style were particularly prominent.

A large grey wolf beat the boys and got away with a sheep for his 4th.

A suggestion from some of the party that it would be a good time to have the brandy keg brought out, but I claimed that as a part of my outfit for medicinal purposes. Gooseberries and chokeberries quite abundant on the bank of the Platt River. At night camped near Wolf Creek. Pleasant.

Tuesday 5th:

Warm this morning. Drove to Castle Creek. Crossed and camped. Wolves numerous. Castle Bluff looms up on the opposite side of the river. Another road on south side. No wood along here and buffalo chips are scarce. Comfortably cool and pleasant.

Wednesday 6th:

Started out early in the morning. Came upon Frazer in his camp. Hot at midday. In the afternoon passed the graves of two young men killed by lightning 12th June. Wolves had dug down to the bodies. Hot and cold winds from showers north and south of us. Trusted the teamsters with the wagons to go ahead and select a camping place. Dark when we got to camp which we found in a low, muddy place infested with mosquitoes, higher land near by. Poor judgment in the selection. Pleasant.

Thursday 7th:

More wolves and rattlesnakes this morning than usual with an occasional hissing viper, garter, green and striped snakes. Tortoises and toads plenty. All seemed out for an airing. Camped near cobble stone bluffs which look like old walls, towers and bastions. Pleasant.

Friday 8th:

Found today as for some days before, wild southernwood, some summer savory and pigweed which are more pungent to take but scent the same as the cultivated. Bluffs are higher. We met a party of Indians. The first for the time since losing our sailor. Showery .

Saturday 9th:

Court House Rock nearly opposite across the Platt. It is three stories high in appearance from the different stratifications. The jail is represented by a square bluff just east of the court house. Dined near river. Drove late. Showers around us but not to reach us. Camped on side of dry bluff. Sheep came in about 10 o'clock.

No water— cook failed to fill the water bags. Supper of crackers and cheese. Wolves howling round us. Clear and pleasant.

Sunday 10th:

Started early to get to water for breakfast which we got nearly north of Chimney Rock south side of river. It is a sandstone shaft, say 50 feet high standing on a conical shaped mound about twice as high. Perhaps it is a hard core left from which the softer rock has been worn away by wind, water and other eroding actions of nature. It is truly named for it stands looking like the smoke stack of a furnace. Many curious shaped bluffs in sight which the imagination may see, forms of animal life "ad libitum". A pack of 12 or 15 wolves hanging round, one fell a victim to a rifle in the hands of Johnson.

Monday 11th:

Came to a trading post and blacksmith shop run by a French Canadian living with Sioux wife or wives. The place is a little way below Scott's Bluff. His prices, $6.00 for shoeing an ox, $1.00 per pair (one foot) for shoes and 4c apiece for nails to put them on with. We had our own so did not have to purchase. Camped opposite to the bluffs which all along are south of the river.

Tuesday 12th:

Drove to Cold Creek in the forenoon. Ben caught some fish with silvery scales and heads much like a trout— very good we found as a pan fish. Made about 12 miles and camped near some strong alkali ponds. Mosquitoes as bad as ever. Pleasant. A Mormon camped with us who had letters for the mail which is sent out from Fort Laramie monthly.

Wednesday 13th:

Passed a halfbreed and Sioux trading post where money is made by picking up lame stock or buying it cheaply and keeping it until it is in good condition and then selling or trading again. Their price, $4.00 to $10.00 for cattle and $1.00 for a sheep if it is fat. Camped by a slough. Pleasant.

Thursday 14th:

Mormon with mail found the carrier from Laramie had left before he arrived so my mail had to wait for the next. Our Mormon express men left us at 3 o'clock P. M. Dined beside the river. A train of 27 Mormon Missionaries met us here—most of them going to Europe. Two men from California also passed, who had left there May 4th. Camped on Rawhide Creek. I shot a big elk. Pleasant.

Friday 15th:

Pressing westward. Another trading post. Indians wearing their summer suits, a breech cloth. Camped on a dry plain with poor feed along the bank of the river. Very hot in the morning. Indians, traders, mountaineers, etc., numerous. Caught a lot of fish out of river.

Saturday 16th:

Drove to the river opposite to Fort Laramie. I crossed to the fort 1 1/2 miles up the Laramie River. The old adobe fort going to ruin—one company of cavalry occupy two old wooden buildings. Officer quarters nearby, two stables and a store all in dilapidated condition. Thermometer 80° in the shade hanging on the adobe wall at noon. Made the ice water kept on hand by the barrel most inviting. *Bodies of dead Indians on scaffolds in trees*, blankets around them.

Sunday 17th:

Drove a few miles to grass and laid by. Mrs. Johnson made some apple pies which were relished by all. Our camp is on a point in the river. 400 head of cattle across the river. 17 horses near us. 2,000 sheep just below us. A stranger with us whose train is 30 miles ahead. Sold Wilson provisions. Cloudy.

Monday 18th:

Struck into the Black Hills. First pines and cedars close by the trail. Some very steep hills—road winding through them. Some of the hills look green, but on approaching them are barren. Camped on the river with very poor feed. Heavy shower at sunset; pleasant after it. Half breed traders or stealers near by.

Tuesday 19th:

Killed a huge yellow rattler. Drove today to Alder Clump at which there is a large spring and a trading post. Had 10 sheep poisoned by eating some poisonous vegetable. Saved five of them by giving them lard. Wolves numerous. They follow on our trail to pick up whatever there may be left when we camp. They watch the birds and when one flies down to the place we have vacated, the wolves immediately bounce in to divide the crumbs or fragments with their winged pilots. Hills on all sides. Pleasant .

Wednesday 20th:

Started early to get the animals away from the place where poison had affected our sheep particularly. Trail good. Grave by the side of the road, child of 7 years. A wild rose and prickly pear protected it to a certain extent from wild animals. Warm at noon. Dined near a creek and drove into dry bluffs. Camped. A man from Oregon travelling alone passed along.

Thursday 21st:

Air cool and bracing in the high rolling country this forenoon. Dined on the river bank. Two large droves of cattle on opposite bank. Heavy showers about 2 o'clock P. M. Passed a series of bluffs which looked like ruins of high walls. Pleasant. 29 large freight wagons loaded are opposite us over the river.

Friday 22nd:

Last night was cold. A man from California 41 days out with pack mules took breakfast with us. Passed a ferry across North Platt this morning. A very heavy shower fell upon us just as we were entering a rough gulch filled with isolated bluffs and bowlders. Drove until about dark and camped on a knoll under a bluff. No grass near.

Saturday 23rd:

After a drive over a rough trail until 10 o'clock A. M. came to feed for our stock. Made camp for the day—concluding to observe a Jewish sabbath. Now making short drives daily. Six men from California camped near us who gave us much information about the route ahead of us. Windy but otherwise pleasant.

Sunday 24th:

Cloudy this morning with a sprinkle of rain. Barren country. Crossed the highest ridge of the Black Hills as they break down at the Platt River. Camped at 2 o'clock on bank of river and swam the oxen and cows across to the Nebraska side for grass. Cattle took a notion to go back east down the river. I crossed in a dugout made from a crooked log evidently for crossing feed to the side we were on, by using two of them with cross poles pinned on the top of each. Cattle got away some 5 miles before I overtook them and drove them back. Johnson came over on horseback to help as I got to bank with them. Saw the finest specimen of Elk that I have ever met, for he came within a hundred feet of me before he stopped and seemed as much interested in me as was desirable. Expecting that I might get upset in the river I had left my weapons in camp, therefore did not want any closer acquaintance. I admired his proud bearing nevertheless. On my attempt to recross the river my dugout struck a snag and overturned, dumping me into the river, so I had to swim for shore pushing my craft ahead of me. The ice cold water chilled me through. It was then the brandy we had along and had not been opened, came in good request. With a liberal drink I rolled up in my blankets and in a little time was in a good perspiration.

Monday 25th:

Felt pretty stiff in the joints. Took an active cathartic. Rode in a wagon. Mrs. Johnson riding my horse. At night felt quite comfortable. The Wilson Brothers came up with us with their flock of sheep Camped in the bluffs on a bed of sand. Cool wolves are very noisy, it seems from their howling that they are without number.

Tuesday 26th:

Took a light breakfast of soda biscuit and buffalo meat. Getting over my cold. Road very rough off and on the bank of the river. Dined on same bill of fare as at breakfast with tea in addition. Fishing much better though my limbs are stiff from my muscular exercise swimming in the ice cold water of the Platt. Cattle got away from us on the road ahead. Could not find them before night. Pleasant.

Wednesday 27th:

Ben, Lewell and Mr. Johnson started at 3 o'clock in the morning after the oxen, following their trail, which we had traced some 7 miles the night before. Returned with them at 3 o'clock P. M. I took care of camp. Had a visit by an Indian and his family who in pantomine tried to let me know that there were bad Indians ahead, but did not fully understand him until next day. Lost a batch of hot biscuits when they left. Bought a riata for a pint cup of sugar. Did not move today. The longest stop since leaving the Missouri River. Pleasant.

Thursday 28th:

Cattle seemed possessed with a roving spirit and would run off at every opportunity. This morning they made a break and swam across the river. I went after them on "Old Nig," a black horse ridden by Mr. Bixby. Don't think the horse was ever before in water when he had to swim, for he went down all under without making an effort to swim until I spurred him severely. Could not get the cattle to take the water on return. Palmer swam across to help me and together we handled them. Palmer got frightened going over, although a good swimmer, having been a sailor on the Lakes, but the undertow scared him, so I crossed and got a rope, in that way towed him across to camp. Old Nig remembering the lesson swam nicely— though this time we found a crossing nearly fordable.

After dinner we drove along until about 3 o'clock with the wagons some distance in the lead, while I was a little in advance of them as usual when I saw a deer ahead and to the right of the trail. Taking a double-barrelled shotgun loaded with revolver bullets I swung off to try for a shot, but I was discovered by the animal and it soon was out of sight. I returned to the road some half a mile or so ahead of the wagons and as I was crossing a little elevation I caught a glimpse of a party of Indians moving through a patch of willow bushes not quite as high as their heads. In an instant and all together they dropped out of sight. There was time however to see that they were moving camp, and Indians, squaws and papooses did not make a rustle even. I remained at my point of observation thinking they would emerge from the brush which came up to the road. The squaws and young ones did not show up, but I think slipped away down the bed of a small stream which was close by.

Presently an old one-eyed mean looking cuss of an Indian with a boy of 15 or 16 years, came up on horseback from quite a different direction from where I had discovered them at first and taking positions each side of me—the boy calling the old one Captain with a motion of his hand towards me as if by way of an introduction. The Captain was armed with a flint lock old English musket and the young one with bow and arrows. The Captain pointing to my Navy pistol said pop, pop, pop. I nodded in the affirmative. I knew the advantage was on my side with a six shooter and double-barrelled gun and percussion caps.

The young scamp commenced to draw up his bow with an arrow intimidatingly—each time a little stronger until I thought it was high time it was stopped lest he might let fly at me. I was more afraid of the arrow than of the musket—therefore mentally decided

54

that if the motion was again made I would shoot him, but made no demonstration or motion to use my revolver whereupon the boy meekly dropped his bow and arrow down by his side. The old Indian moved a little higher up the hill and holding his musket a few seconds at "present arms" brought it down and put some powder into the pan of the lock. I made some signs to Ben and Lewell who were some distance behind with the men with the sheep when the Captain and boy started to meet them.

When the wagons arrived I told them to drive to a level place nearly opposite the brush where the Indian party was seen and stop for the arrival of the rest of the men with the sheep. Soon after halting an half dozen Indians bounced out of the brush and commenced to pillage the wagons.

The teamsters Johnson, Palmer and Jennings were scared out of their wits and offered no resistance but Mrs. Johnson went after their hands with a hatchet when they went to help themselves to things in her wagon.

I found it was necessary for me to put on airs, so went to the wagons scolding the teamsters and ordering the Indians by signs to put everything back they had taken from the wagons. They were sulky and one of them taking an ox yoke bow he had taken by the ends made a motion to strike me with it whereupon I brought my pistol to bear upon him with the intention of shooting when he dropped the bow and every one of them got off to the opposite side of their horses. Then I knew that I was master of the situation. Furthermore I knew they were not prepared for a fight as if they were, they would not have their squaws and papooses along with them. We waited until the men with the sheep came up to us and got all of us around for it being a warm day the men had put their weapons into the wagons excepting Ben and Lewell, who from my signals surmised something was wrong; when my first two Indians approached them they put their pistols under their clothing with just a little of them in sight. The other men did the same with their clothing but had no weapons yet the Indians supposed they had, probably.

After we were all armed I felt better able to manage affairs, though I knew by the experience that four of our party could not be depended upon in a fight.

Two more Indians joined those already present—one of them with a certificate that they were Good Indians. It was written in faultless penmanship expressing the hope we would treat them well so we gave them some hardtack and a sheep that was lame. They did not seem satisfied.

After we had got our train in close order we told the boys to start ahead; as they moved the old one-eyed Captain said to his Indians in Spanish that they would not let us go until they had the black cow and the sheep that had bells on, and told his boy to go ahead and stop us. The boy started and when nearly ahead we told him in Spanish to come back. As he started to obey the command the old one- eyed Captain called him derisively a boy and said he would stop the train until they had what they wanted. He started and when part way round we levelled our rifles on him and told him to come back; he hesitated a little but came back to where the other Indians were.

As we were moving on the old Captain got down on one knee and levelled his gun at us which frightened two of our men so, they ran for shelter, much to the delight of the Indians. Just at that time a report came that the black cow was missing. Supposing the Indians had slipped out of the brush and cut her out we made a rush for the Indian when they rushed into the brush for shelter. Then it was out turn to laugh as the cow was only a little way off when found browsing. The Indians were very greatly surprised when they found we could use the Spanish language. We found that they were a hunting and marauding party of Arapahoes from Texas and the Indian visitor of yesterday was not friendly with them. In the party we learned there were about 90 young and old.

We drove some six miles and camped on a round knoll away from brush and gulches with the stock all around us, for our men could see Indians everywhere. Windy.

Friday 29th:

No disturbance during the night and there was no sleeping on guard.

Passed a bridge across the Platt—a very strong one built of hewn timbers. Reported to have cost $14,000. All trains on south side of the Platt cross here to north side. Camped on bank of river 3 or 4 miles above the bridge in a large bottom extending back from river bank—18 miles above the bridge there is a ford at this season of the year. Found a nitrous deposit on a hill, a kind of a lake bed on summit. Pleasant.

Saturday 30th:

Followed up the Platt River to the point where we leave it for good and halted for dinner. Horses stampeded, frightened by a trader's wagon carrying a flag. They ran back to a camp about 3 miles behind us. Took in wood and water and drove out a few miles on an alkali plain. Showers in the afternoon but pleasant at night. Getting along all right. Supplied some Mormon families with provisions to take them to Salt Lake City, they having been robbed by the Good Indians. 5 families of foreigners, mostly English. The women said they were prodded with arrows to make them to hurry up the cooking for them.

Sunday 31st:

Mr. Jennings gave us a scare on his guard by shooting at what he supposed to be an Indian creeping into camp, but it proved to be a sheep that had strayed. It was a good long shot but he hit his mark and killed the sheep. Our men have been very timid since the man was killed from our party. Broke camp for Willow Springs. No good water between the Platt and the Springs. Passed Avenue Rocks and Poison Springs, arriving at Willow Springs about 10 o'clock P. M. Camped. No grass. 700 miles from the Missouri River. An uncomfortable place. Clear and cold.

August—Monday 1st:

Started at sunrise. Drove to Greasewood Creek where we found feed for our stock and camped for the night. Weather pleasant and cool, though windy and rainy in P. M.

Had a sage hen for supper. A large species of grouse nearly the size of a turkey. Cows ran away with a drove passing us and had some trouble getting them back as the party passing claimed them as strays.

Tuesday 2nd:

Travelled leisurely along to the Sweetwater River and drove up near to Independence Rock a large oblong granite boulder about 650 yards long and forty in height entirely bare except a little spot on top in a depression where there was a few shrubs and a solitary pine. It was named "Rock Independence" by a party of explorers camped there on 4th July, about 1840. Many names of explorers are painted on the Rock. Latitude 42° 29' 36". Fremont August 1, 1842. Passed on the way a high granite bluff. Camped on a bench overlooking the valley where our stock were turned out to feed. Numerous alkali lakes northeast of camp where crystalized carbonate of soda of unknown depth shows on surface like snow ice and when dug into looks clear as ice. We shovelled out a hole the depth of a spade handle and filled a grain sack with it for future use.

Wednesday 3rd:

Did not move today so as to let our animals recruit a little. Had to keep guard over the animals because they would scatter in feeding, hunting for best grass. Ben and John Trust fishing but caught nothing. Some fish to be had at the trading post near by. Lewell and I more lazy than the others stayed in the tent reading and snoozing. Mrs. Johnson did some washing. 3 of our horses stampeded at dark. Ben followed them but returned at 11 o'clock without them. Pleasant.

Thursday 4th:

Ben left at sunrise in pursuit of horses. Found them 30 miles back on the road caught by a company bringing a lot of horses through to California. Lost 7 sheep from poison. Sent a letter to be mailed at Fort Laramie to Dr. Gould by a mountaineer with whom I swapped a blanket for a buffalo robe. At 2 o'clock moved camp. Passed Devil's Gate and made camp for the night.

Friday 5th:

Followed the bank of the Sweetwater. Passed Devil's Gate entrance to a rough, deep canon to the north of the trail in the Wind River range of mountains and on south are the Green River Mountains. The former nearly bare granite, the latter wooded on summits and sides. Camped near an alkali lake. Pleasant and cool as usual along here.

Saturday 6th:

At noon I climbed a nearby peak of the mountains from which the snowy summits of the Rocky Mountains could be seen. Found rugged and deep canons into which I fired my pistol several times to hear the reverberations rattle among the crags like thunder. Found some ripe, wild gooseberries which came in very opportunely to quake my thirst. They were smooth and of a deep garnet color. Gathered some for seed. In the afternoon passed some peculiar bluffs of various colors. Camped in the valley of the Sweetwater. Pleasant.

Sunday 7th:

The feed being poor did not stop at noon but drove 11 miles and camped in good grass. Windy in the P. M. raising a thick dust which was decidedly unpleasant for those driv- ing sheep. Met the Salt Lake 4-horse mail stage east bound. Clear weather.

Monday 8th:

Moved on leisurely. Took dinner on the bank of the Sweetwater and let our animals lay in food and water for a 17 miles drive in soft sand. Here Mr. Biddell, U. S. Indian Agent for Utah passed us from Warsaw, Illinois since July 4th. At 2 o'clock the wind blew almost a hurricane for 15 minutes piling the sand into drifts. Snow-capped peaks of the Rockies between us and sunset and to the east a splendid rainbow, which of course was preceeded by a shower. Camped on an open plain.

Tuesday 9th:

Struck camp at sunrise. Moved on, hoping to find feed. Drove to Ford No. 6. Some poor grass. Stopped for dinner. Remained here over night. Mr. Johnson sick. Now the Sweetwater looks like a New England brook—clear water with rocky bottom. No fish but suckers. Pleasant but cool at night.

August 10th:

Pleasant. Mr. Johnson still ill. Lewell with his team. Took dinner at Ford No. 7 Sweetwater. Air full of grasshoppers, partially obscuring the sun. Road leaves river for a long distance. On my watch I cooked some ducks for breakfast time. Found strawberries on a creek by that name.

Thursday 11th:

Passed today the Soapsuds Lakes. Three of them. Road hilly and ledgy in places in forenoon's drive. Camped on Quaking Asp Creek, so called from the species of poplars on its banks, the leaves of which move in the slightest breeze. Johnson still on sick list. Snow peaks of Rocky Mountains close by. Pleasant. Warmest night that we have had for a long time.

Friday 12th:

The warm temperature of last night modifies the cool air from the snowy summits, makes delightful mornings. Breakfasted on beans cooked in the ground, a hole heated and filled in with the coals, with tea, coffee, bacon, warm bread, pepper sauce and pickles. Dined at Ford No. 9 Sweetwater. Elk and antelope getting scarce. Johnson better. Had cold beans, bread, etc., from breakfast cooking. Drove out 7 miles expecting to find feed to camp on. according to Horn's guide book. Found none so camped in sage brush on sand. All hands growling about the uncertainty of guides.

Saturday 13th:

Up and off early. Soon bid adieu to waters that flow to the Atlantic and crossed the summit of the South Pass in the Rocky Mountains and drank from Pacific Springs the head water of the Colorado River of the West which flows into the Gulf of California. Camped at lower end of the first bog. Sheep could feed on the bog by keeping them from getting huddled together; if they did the sod would give away and they would sink with it into the water— cattle, horses had dry picking on the outside. At night we could hear beavers fling into the air holes their flat tails, striking like a board on the surface. Light showers passing along the ridges. Grey wolves numerous. Brilliant meteors seen on my watch—9 to 12 o'clock P. M.

Sunday 14th:

Drove today over barren waste. No water or grass. After making about 16 miles camped. Wolves plenty. They stole my whip and ate it, leaving only the stock. Cattle and sheep uneasy for want of grass and water. Fed our horses a little meal. Warm and pleasant.

August—Monday 15th:

Johnson better today and drove his team a part of the day. Palmer spilled most of the water we had taken along for breakfast coffee, into the fire. Being the last one on guard it was a part of his duty to heat water as a starter for the morning meal. This caused some cuss words and long faces. Enough was saved for a pot of tea.

About 11 o'clock reached the Little Sandy. Cool forenoon as usual because at night the wind changes and blows from the snow-capped mountains. Was overtaken here by a Mormon train of seven small wagons. Took dinner and moved down river 3 miles to good feed for stock.

Tuesday 16th:

Laid by to recruit a little. Sold Mormons a 50 pound sack of flour, calculated to be enough with what they had to take them to Salt Lake City. Snow-capped mountains to northwest and south of us. Water cold from melting snow. We shot a dozen sage hens and chickens among us. This bird is a large species of the grouse family and good eating. Cool at night as usual but pleasant at night though windy in the afternoon.

Wednesday 17th:

Arrived at Big Sandy (river) in the forenoon. Found good feed for sheep and laid by until 3 o'clock P. M. Started out for a drive of 17 miles from Big Sandy across a desolate country. Camped at 9 o'clock. Wind blowing a gale directly in our faces all the afternoon filled with dust. Calculated to start by 3 or 4 o'clock in the morning. Clear —not very cold. Indians in sight. None came into camp.

Thursday 18th:

Through the negligence of the last guard we were not called until 5 o'clock this morning, giving us the prospect of a long drive under a hot midday sun to strike the river again, which made us all cross, etc. Struck the river about 2 o'clock and camped. Feed for sheep, none for the other animals. Showers passed around us and light clouds at night.

Friday 19th:

Drove to Green River—properly named from the color of its waters. Some 50 settlers below the lower ferry where we are, composed of hunters, Indian traders, frontier desperadoes, etc. Some rice at 35c per lb. Tea at $1.25 and a few other articles at same rate of prices. 4 or 5 houses and blacksmith shop here. Camped. Had a shower with hail towards night. Pleasant afterward. All O. K.

Saturday 20th:

Could not make a trade with the ferry owner that we thought reasonable, he evidently thinking we would have to come to his terms because sheep were not swimmers. We reconnoitered a little way below and found a place where we could ford by raising the wagon beds a little and the current set across to opposite side, so taking advantage of the current the sheep followed the wagons with a little urging and swam across nicely about 200 feet from bank to bank. Found good grass on the west bank so camped to give the stock chance to recruit a little for we had had a desert drive of 75 miles. Pleasant weather.

Sunday 21st:

Some mountaineer visitors enjoying their own voices very much, especially as they made our boys 'eyes bulge out with narratives of hair breadth escapes, etc. Found by three dead sheep and as many cows of our Mormon fellow travellers that we were in midst of poisonous weeds, so pulled out and down river about 9 miles and camped on a bluff near a grassy bottom on which there were some Mormons camped. Had a rattle with Indian dogs that were hungry for a feed on mutton. Cross, Livingston and Co.'s train with merchandise for Salt Lake City arove in their camp. Pleasant.

Monday 22nd:

Sheep in a contrary mood and hard to guard. Started at 10 o'clock to drive across south of main trail across the bluffs to Black's Fork, about 6 miles to grass. Found an abundance of bunch grass all along to the Fork. Good feed for cattle and horses but we kept the sheep out of the bottom. Frosty on Green River. Pleasant in the afternoon. The Livingston train got across ahead of us.

Tuesday 23nd:

Started up Black's Fork. Found our cut off is making the 15 miles much longer, but there has been no lack of feed. Drove to where the main trail strikes the Fork and camped for the night. Water muddy—a small stream. As convenient camp for sheep as have had for a long time. Pleasant.

Wednesday 24th:

Moved out in good season, letting the sheep on the bunch grass which grows on the side of the bluffs. Water still muddy. Crossed Harris Fork, a beautiful clear stream with water of a greenish color. Dined on Black Fork and started out at 4 o'clock. Camped in the sage brush in a barren kind of an amphitheatre opening out on the Fork.

Thursday 25th:

Broke camp at 4 o'clock A. M. Pleasant but cold. So had our coats buttoned up tight and close, being the coldest morning we have had this side of the South Pass. Jim Palmer and John Trust had a regular squaw fight. At ten o'clock camped for the day on a small creek. Hildreth's flock passed us. Met a pack train from Volcano, California. Windy and cold. Pleasant. Hard work to keep the stock together, the night being dark and stock hungry. Moon after midnight.

Friday 26th:

Being well refreshed, man and beast, we started for Bridgers Fort[15] about 4 o'clock in the morning. John feeling mad, packed up, intending to leave us but by keeping Jim's gun from him concluded to remain as we had taken his gun also. He said, "By tarn I can't go way mit out my gun." Hot day. Road to the Fort longer than we expected, but about sundown the stock began to smell water which proved to be about 3 miles off and they rushed for it, covering the intervening distance in short time comparatively. Struck the water about 1 mile below the Fort. Distance 20 miles instead of 14 as we supposed. Camped on a small bottom. All hands tired.

Saturday 27th:

Moved to a small creek bottom with our sheep for feed, opposite to the fort and to avoid poisonous weeds that grew in the larger bottoms in which Hildreth lost 13 sheep just below our last camping place. White went to the Fort for ammunition but found the Fort in possession of the territorial officer. Mormons who had 24 hours before driven old man Bridger out and taken possession. Fort made by setting in the ground two parallel lines of high posts and filling in between with gravelly clay. The location commanded

---

[15] Now Fort Bridger State Historic Site, in Wyoming.

quite an extensive view of surrounding country. Here Bridger had established his trading post many years before his fort had been taken by the Mormons[16], with a goodly supply of merchandise selected for the Indian trade.

At 2 o'clock started out on the trail. Rainy and cold. At the end of about 8 miles drove into a deep gulch in a high ridge. Altitude 6,700 feet where there was good grass and water. Camped. Pleasant at midnight. Range of snow-capped mountains on the south.

Sunday 28th:

8 o'clock A. M. Am sitting on the lee side of a large sage bush with a cold wind at my back. Cattle, sheep and horses feeding in the gulch and on its sides. The smoke from our camp fire rises perpendicularly to the top of the bluffs before catching the wind. Very little wood in sight except some pines near the snow belt. Drove to Muddy Fork 4 miles. Camped on a small bottom near a soda spring, deep and muddy giving out a sulphur smell. Rainy.

Monday 29th:

Started out early. Crossed a ridge 7,315 feet altitude. Drove along the ridge to next summit and dined on the side. Here found a camp of 40 Mormons out hunting Indians and to assist their emigrants. 40 more at Fort Bridger. In the afternoon crossed the summit 7,700 feet altitude. Highest point on trail of the Wasatch Mountains and the divide between the waters of the Colorado River and of the Great Salt Lake basin. Having driven 15 miles, camped on Sulphur Creek. Pleasant and cold.

---

[16] In 1843

Tuesday 30th:

Snow near by. Water in spring close to camp very cold from melting snow. Another very strong with sulphur. Coal near by. Oil spring reported to be about a mile away. Wrote a short letter to father.

Started on our journey crossing Bear River in the morning. Took our dinner in a small valley where we found the best grass since leaving Green River. Short drive today. More Mormons. Camped on a grassy bottom. Pleasant weather.

Wednesday 31st:

Our drive this morning is down Yellow Creek past some curious conglomerate bluffs. Dined at the foot of a steep grade which we surmounted in the afternoon and found quite a change in the landscape. Hills covered with grass, trees and shrubs the first since crossing the Missouri River. Showery. Camped in Echo Canon, opposite Cache Cave—a small oven like shaped cave in the sand rock bluff in which many a traveller had inscribed his name and we did likewise.

September—Thursday 1st:

Following down Echo Canon[17]. The report of a pistol shot would reverberate from crag to crag until it would seem to die away in the distance. Perpendicular bluff on right hand side going down—on left somewhat sloping. Average width about 20 rods. Length 21 1/2 miles with a gradual descent. Camped on creek in the canon opposite to some very high perpendicular bluffs.

---

[17] Utah

Friday 2nd:

Still on the creek in the canon. Higher bluffs on the sides as the creek strikes Weber River. Red and grey sandstone and red conglomerate filled with pebbles as if with cement. Took dinner on Weber River near a vacant house —more in sight down the river, all uninhabited. Deserted, it is said, on account of Indian attacks, so were called in to Salt Lake City by order of Brigham Young. Crossed the river and camped on a moist bottom on the southeasterly side. Pleasant.

Saturday 3rd:

Remained in camp this forenoon. Caught a few trout and White shot some ducks so we had a variety for dinner. In P. M. drove over the mountain 5 1/2 miles. On the summit had splendid view of Mountains around and beneath us. The westerly descent in a narrow ravine. Had to drive late to find a place smooth enough to camp on, finally came to one in a patch of brush. Trail very rough—a sprinkle of a shower.

Sunday 4th:

About midnight a large bear made its presence, probably attracted by hope of a mutton for breakfast. Lewell being on guard he wisely drove it away without making an alarm. Moved camp to Canon Creek for feed where we remained for the remainder of the day. About sunset I saw a calf wandering around and went to drive it to camp with the sheep. It started away from me and I followed, as I thought, the sound it made in the brush but on nearing an open space the boys in camp cried out, "a bear, a bear!" and I discovered that I had been trailing a bear, the calf having turned aside. It was not a large one. Mr. Johnson grabbed the best rifle and ran after the bear which had gone into the creek nearby. As he reached the bank the bear raised upon its hind feet almost under him. Johnson took to his heels when all hands shouted, "shoot, shoot!" He banged away but his rifle pointed skyward as I could see, but he averred that he hit the bear. Had he been in less haste and waited for assistance we might have had bear steak for breakfast. The bear retreated a little way into some thick brush where our shepherd dog, Watch, held it at bay some time, but we thought it prudent not to go after it. Johnson's bravery was the subject of ridicule in camp thereafter.

Monday 5th:

Drove on up the creek which is in a deep canon until noon. Took dinner and drove to the summit of another ridge in the mountains and camped in sight of the Great Salt Lake Valley. Snow covered peaks to the south of us. High cragged mountains on either hand. Am somewhat indisposed from headache last night. Pleasant.

Tuesday 6th:

Found a lot of Mormons with teams here hauling wood and lumber for the valley.

Descending from our mountain camp by a very steep grade into another deep canon, followed it down some 8 miles where we found feed for our stock, the first for 24 hours, and to be the last, as we were informed, for the next 20 miles. Camped until tomorrow. Pleasant.

Wednesday 7th:

Crossed the last ridge before entering the valley of the Great Salt Lake and descended into a canon through which we travelled 7 miles and emerged from Emigrant Canon, as it is called, upon a high tableland 5 miles from Salt Lake City. Deserted cabins all along the trail from last night's camp. The settlers having been ordered into city by Brigham Young on account of alleged hostile Indians. As we were driving along two men on horseback met us and one of them asked me if we were "Saints or sinners." I replied that it depended very much how he interpreted the question, when he said somewhat testily, "Are you Mormons or not?" Not was the reply. They then asked what train it was and I told him; upon that they wheeled about and rode off toward the city. In a short time two more men came out and meeting us said, "We know who you are. You are the ones that assisted some of our people on the plains who had been robbed by the Indians. You may turn off to the left and go down the hill to the church gardens and camp there until you hear from us again—but keep your stock off the plowed lands." Camped near a garden patch and by invitation helped ourselves to whatever vegetable we liked which was a great treat. Our horses were taken to a feed yard in the city. Word was sent us that if we could go to a certain house in the city, we would be repaid in kind for what we had furnished their people whom we had befriended on the plains.

Thursday 8th:

Drove to the city, went to the place designated and got the provisions that we had traded to the Mormons back on the trail, not knowing that we would ever hear from them again, but we found it a very good turn of affairs in our favor, for we were kindly received and treated wherever we went. It was our intention to drive to the north of the city and perhaps camp for the winter, but meeting a Mr. Wilson, by his advice turned back south for a better camp on the River Jordan which runs into Salt Lake from Lake Provo. Fed our oxen and horses in the city and in the afternoon drove out 8 miles and camped near a Mr. Caspars of whom we bought feed for oxen and horses, paying him $1.25 per dozen sheaves of oats. Dined on green corn from the church cornfield.

Friday 9th:

Started south again. At morning were ordered off from unoccupied ground on the pretext that it was a neighborhood range. Did not move and nothing more said. In the afternoon struck Willow Creek and camped at Warm Springs, a poor place but could do no better. Pleasant.

Saturday 10th:

Moved off early hoping to find feed for sheep as there was none here, save what was fenced in. Outside there was nothing but a miserable yellow weed which the stock would not eat.

Sunday 11th:

Moved a few miles to the banks of the Jordan in Utah Valley where we found plenty good feed and intend to remain a week or two. Here we found Mr. Frazer who had been here with his train some days. Plenty of green corn, squash, melons, potatoes, etc., which was most enjoyable to all in contrast with the barren plains we had passed over. Fish plenty and of good quality of various kinds.

Monday 12th:

Ben and I went to the city with Mr. Wilson to lay in some necessary articles for the camp also to try the cattle market for it is our intention to purchase about 100 head of oxen. Arrived early in the evening and put up at Bro. Hawkins. Pleasant weather.

Tuesday 13th:

In the city taking observations. Saw Brigham on the streets. Did not call upon him. Paid our respects to the wives of Francis M. Pomroy, fulfilling a promise made to one of his father-in-laws whom we had met back on the Platt River. This Mr. Pomroy was from the State of Maine. Bought a few cattle. Obtained some buffalo robes and retired as the night before to a hay stack in preference to an upper room in a crowded hotel.

Wednesday 14th:

Circulating among the Mormons yet buying cattle. Paying from $60 to $90 per yoke which is cheaper than they could have been purchased in Illinois because of the Indian difficulties which prevents the occupation of the cattle ranges. Pleasant.

Thursday 15th:

Ben and I with a new hand, Robert Mack, left Salt Lake City to drive the cattle we have on hand to our camp on the Jordan. Purchased some more on the way. Stopped for the night on Big Cottonwood with a Mormon with two wives. They gave us a good supper. We herded our cattle in a small field keeping guard outside, sleeping as we could catch a nap in our blankets, but a shower coming up in the night made it very uncomfortable.

Friday 16th:

Bought more cattle of our host (2 yoke of oxen and one cow) and started for our camp again. Dallied along looking at stock, bought some, finally struck a Mr. Dillon from Illinois with 210 sheep that were sound and a few cattle. Bought the sheep at $4 per head. I started with cattle for camp and Ben returned to city to close up some unfinished business. Reached camp at midnight. Driving at night against Brigham's advice.

Saturday 17th:

Returned to Dillon's camp, a distance of 18 miles where I met Ben. Took the 210 sheep, 2 yoke of oxen and 4 cows, paying $1,040.00 for the lot and drove across to a Mr. Rose's where we are to get another yoke of oxen. Put our stock into a leaky corral where we had to lay by and watch them all night. Pleasant but cold.

Sunday 18th:

Heavy frost last night nevertheless we had a ghostly apparition in the shape of a lanky woman in her night clothes who made inquiry for her cows. Drove to home camp. Well tired out, having had little sleep for 4 nights.

Monday 19th:

Resting in camp. Wrote a letter to father. Our men taking care of the stock around us which appear to enjoy the good grazing we have placed them on. Ben and I relieved Lewell of the care of the camp he has had for a week. Pleasant weather.

Tuesday 20th:

Lewell is gone to the city 30 miles. Some of the men fishing, hunting, mending clothes, taking care of the stock, etc. Much company. Mormons and emigrants, the latter like ourselves, bound for California.

Wednesday 21st:

In camp. Ben and I made a fine catch of fish. Some very fine trout with chubs graced our string. At night a Mormon with two wives who drove their horses so hard that they gave out to get across the mountains six miles from us as they feared an attack from Indians at the pass. We have not seen Indians that gave us any fear of disturbance.

Thursday 22nd:

Still in camp waiting for Lewell to get back from Salt Lake City who made his appearance soon after noon. All hands glad to see him as we want to be moving south by short daily drives. Pleasant weather.

Friday 23rd:

Up and moving as early as we could, but it is something like breaking up housekeeping and repacking everything, took considerable time. Passed Dry Creek settlement and camped just south of American Fork settlement. Both places fortified and forted up as they called [it,] by a square enclosure made of logs set into the ground close together, about 12 feet from the ground to the top. A gateway guarded by sentries every night prevented ingress or egress without permission of the Bishop. In the center was a corral into which the stock was driven at sunset and driven out upon the range and guarded daily lest the Indians might stampede them as it is reported by the Mormons, numbers of whom are in camp offering to barter for worn out sheep, groceries or anything. Pleasant.

Saturday 24th:

Detained in camp waiting for a Mormon who promised to come early to trade some flour for worn out sheep. Did not trade with him after all. So started for Provo City. Passed near that place and camped on the River Provo, 1 1/2 miles above—near a deserted farm. I rode into town and contracted for 1,000 lbs. of flour at $6.00 per hundred and some beef at $9.00 per hundred lbs.

Sunday 25th:

Remained in camp to have some blacksmith work done on the wagons. I rode past Spring Creek settlement to where Frazer was camped—some 7 miles. Late in getting back to our camp but found at the shop that they were just setting the wagon wheel tires. By Brigham's order the Mormons pay no attention to keeping Sunday until their fortifications are completed and harvesting done. Light rains today but pleasant at night. Exchanged some coffee for butter. Nothing else would be accepted in exchange. Coin was of no account to them.

Monday 26th:

Got under way after considerable delay. John Trust, the Dutchman, and White, the blacksmith talked of leaving the train and no men to be had nearer than the city 48 miles off. They finally concluded to remain with us. Just at starting Reuben Percy Mack joined us on horseback. Had some trouble in getting across the river. Drove through Provo taking on the flour and beef in passing, paying for them in coffee, pepper and spices at 40c per lb. We camped on Little Spring Creek 2 miles from the town. Pleasant.

Tuesday 27th:

Drove on today past Spring Creek Settlement and to the right of Palmyra and camped on a creek from which water was taken to irrigate the land. Some of the ditch crossings were very miry therefore hard to get through, especially for the sheep. Pleasant but cold nights.

Wednesday 28th:

Pushed on this morning—passing White and Viles' train in camp to Peeteneet Settlement, made a short stop and bought a cask to salt beef in, cost $5. On arriving at Frazer's camp we pitched our tent for the night. Ben and Lewell returned to town and bought 4 oxen and steers which they drove to camp. Pleasant.

Thursday 29th:

Started out quite early. Frazer's train ahead, ours next. White and Viles following and Judge Burdick's in the rear, who came up just as we were breaking camp. Crossed the summit between Utah and Salt Creek valleys where we were informed at starting that we might expect trouble from the Indians. It was reported that one of Tom Hildreth's men had been robbed there. We camped between the Deep Springs and Willow Creek. Springs 80 or 40 feet deep. Willow Creek the Mormons reported no one passed without an attack but not an Indian put in an appearance.

Friday 30th:

Moved the sheep some time in advance. Found few had picked up poison of some kind. One died, the other we saved by pouring down their throats warm lard. Drove through Salt Creek settlement and camped where there was no feed. Pleasant but cold.

October—Saturday 1st:

More delay and trouble. Bought some potatoes of a Mormon who was not on time in delivering them, so left Ben and Jennings with team to get them while the rest of us moved on to Tulare Creek and camped. It was late when Ben and Jennings came in. Before starting this morning Frazer got a left hand benefit from the Mormons of Naphi. They drove his horses into their corral and fined him $20 costs and damages, alleging they had strayed to their wheat stacks but would not show him the damage, threatened to double the amount if he found fault or swore .

Sunday 2nd:

Drove to Sevier River and camped on a point made by a crook in the stream. Frazer on another. White and Viles and the Judge on still another further down. Good feed. Pleasant and cool as usual.

Monday 3rd:

Started out early. Had to cross the river. Water so deep that it came up over the axles of the wagons. Bad crossing for sheep on account of high steep bank on opposite side. The bridge had been washed away. Drove some 13 miles from the river which terminated in lake Sevier (where a party of U. S. Engineers was killed a short time after we passed[18]). Camped in Round Valley. Frazer here joined our party to drive along together—thereby doubling our guard at night to prevent thieving Indians from stampeding our horses and cattle. Sheep if frightened would huddle around the camp fire but the other stock would run away and scatter more or less.

Tuesday 4th:

Travelled over the divide between Round Valley and the main valley which extends southerly from Great Salt Lake, a long drive without water. Mrs. Johnson quite ill and has been two or three days. Drove to Cedar Creek and Spring and camped in a barren valley. No fish in the stream. Pleasant and warm.

Wednesday 5th:

Crossed Pioneer Creek soon after starting out. Had 15 sheep die from some kind of poison—a great many more on the ground in spasms. I discovered something was wrong from seeing so many carcasses and rushed back and had the flock hurried across as quickly as possible. Col. Hollister lost 86 head out of about 4,000-—a larger proportion than our loss. His train was a day's drive ahead of us. After a short drive from the creek we came to Fillmore, the capitol of the territory of Great Salt Lake. Camped and waited for the flock to get upon their feet and come up to us. Here we found Ed. Potter from Col. Hollister's train. Dined with him at Bishop Bartholmew's. Potter came back to assist two girls to join Colonel's train, with it come to California and return by

---

[18] On the 26th of October 1853, members of the corps of Topographical Engineers on the Pacific Railway Survey. Captain J. W. Gunnison and seven of his men were killed by Pah Ute Indians.

water to Ohio as they refused to join the Mormons. Mrs. Bartholmew being a saint and the bishop their stepfather who proposed to have them sealed to him as celestial wives. Potter arranged with the consent of the mother that they should ride in the wagon with Mrs. Johnson to overtake Hollister's train who would hold up for them the next day. We went into camp nearby the town.

Thursday 6th:

In the morning the girls came out to milk their cows and told us that the old folks had concluded not to let them go East that way but they were promised that in the Spring they might leave with some of the Mormon trains that would go east at that time with Mormon missionaries. So Potter rode away to overtake his train.

After purchasing a few necessary articles we drove 8 miles to Chalk Creek. Frazer killed a small beef of which we have one-half to be repaid when we kill. It is a very warm day. Hollister's train 12 miles ahead. Road very dusty.

Friday 7th:

Took a late and leisurely start and drove to Corn Creek or Willow Flat, 4 miles. As Mr. Burnap and I were selecting a place for camp an Indian came up and showed us water and feed. He soon left us and returning brought in Capt. Connuse and party of about a dozen Indians. Next move they sent for their squaws. All of whom we out of friendship had to feed. This same party had killed one of Hildreth's men who was trying to disarm the Captain. Hildreth's men in turn killed an Indian and wounded two, camped near the Indian wickeups.

Saturday 8th:

Crossed over a ridge to a small round valley without water, then over another ridge to a spring 25 miles from our last night's camp. All hands tired. Stock wearied. Warm day. Roads dusty. Poor watering place. Feed good. Supper over all hands excepting the guard turned in. Pleasant weather.

Sunday 9th:

Laid by to rest stock and ourselves as much as possible, though it is about as hard work on the men as driving. White, Judge Burdick & Co., drive on. Windy with a little rain in the afternoon. Pleasant at night though cool. Mr. Burnap and I go ahead of the train nowadays to select camping places.

Monday 10th:

Started again, when about two miles out met Lewell coming back from the sheep which were as usual in the lead, having lost his Colts Revolver went back to our camping place in search for it, but did not find it. We overtook the train in camp some six miles from last camp in good place, recruiting for a drive of 16 or 22 miles tomorrow. Pleasant.

Tuesday 11th:

Sheep started before sunrise. Cattle grazed for a short time and started, crossed a high ridge. New snow on a mountain near by. Mountain scenery to the east of us very grand. Frazer's teamster broke down a wagon wheel when about six miles on our way. Delayed about 2 hours putting a skid in place of the wheel. Camped at 7 o'clock on Sage Creek. A miserable watering place as the water ran in a deep gulch. No feed. Pleasant.

Wednesday 12th:

Started as early as we could see to pack up. Drove 5 miles to Beaver Creek and laid by for the day. A good place. Mended the wheel. Mountains all around us. Clear cold night.

Thursday 13th:

Had a long tedious drive today without feed or water. At sunset arrived at a small spring of water and a plat of poor grass where we camped. Cattle troublesome from want of water but had to stand it with very little of it. Cold and pleasant.

Friday 14th:

Left our inconvenient quarters early for the next creek about 5 miles ahead. On reaching it we camped. Ben and Frazer went into Parowan City to purchase some supplies needed to last us until we should arrive in California. Overtook White & Co., resting in camp. Poor feed. Pleasant weather.

Saturday 15th:

Laid by to recruit. I, as usual bossed the making of a stew, after the preliminary for it had been accomplished by the men. Seven miles yet to Parowan, the last settlement in Great Salt Lake Valley.

Found a party of Mormons had arrested Potter for seduction of the two girls at Filmore. They had attempted to do it a few days previous but he slipped away from them, mounted his horse and they were not able to catch him—his horse being the fleetest. This time they got ahead of him and laid for him in a canebrake through which the road ran. They talked of taking him to Salt Lake City for trial but we were strong enough to say No. As there were some 60 men in the three trains that had stopped there, we were at least for the time, master of the situation. Word was sent to Col. Hollister that if he thought best we would send the posse back and take Potter along with us. The Mormons however were only on a raid, so trumped up the charge and were ready to make terms. It was arranged that a fine of $300 would answer of which $150 would be allowed for the horse that they could not catch when Potter gave them the slip, and $150 cash. By that time our party had got up quite a warlike feeling and wanted Col. Hollister to refuse the offer so that we could have a chance at the Mormon posse of seven men, but the Col. accepted and thus the matter was settled; the leader of the posse giving a U. S. receipt and discharging Potter, turned with his men.

Ben and Frazer are in Parowan.

Sunday 16th:

Arrived in Parowan the last fortified city in the valley and the most southerly of the Mormon settlements—pleasantly located at the foot of a mountain range on the east side of Little Salt Lake Valley, a clear stream of water running in ditches in the front and back of the houses. One for house use, the other for stock and the public. A square corral in the center into which all the stock belonging to the city was driven at night for safety and control of the church officers. All affairs here as elsewhere being under church direction. Camped just east of the city. Pleasant.

Monday 17th:

Traded some with the Mormons—groceries for butter, cheese, etc. Had some blacksmithing done by a Mr. Whitney, originally from Maine. Mailed a letter to father and one to Postmaster Grant, Salt Lake, requesting all letters, if any to be forwarded to Los Angeles. In afternoon drove to a small creek 8 miles out and camped. Pleasant. Five wagons of Mormons going out for California, joined us here, requested the privilege of travelling with us. Their stock very troublesome at night but not one of the men would go out to look after them at night—it was said for fear of the "'Destroying Angels."

Tuesday 18th:

A young Indian calling himself Mike invited himself to stay with us. Drove to Coal Creek or Little Muddy.

Passed Johnson Springs, a very pleasant farm but now deserted, as the occupants were ordered to go into the fort at Parowan. We helped ourselves to garden vegetables in variety. Camped near by. Pleasant.

Wednesday 19th:

Drove to Iron Springs and creek where we camped. Boulders of Magnetic Iron ore laying around in abundance. Barren country all around. Little bunch grass. Train of 17 wagons of disappointed Mormons left here this morning for California before we did. Cloudy.

Thursday 20th:

A clear cold autumn morning with piercing wind. Indians call it **coch wino** (very bad). Travelled over a barren road. No feed, but sagebrush. Came to a spring in the side of a mountain, scarcely enough water for our use. Some scattering bunch grass on the foot of the mountain. A kind of valley without water. Mike, the Indian decamped about 10 o'clock and with him went a powder horn, blanket, and a piece of carpeting. The men on guard were instructed to keep a close watch on him every night, but he gave them a slip.

Friday 21st:

Grazed the stock the best we could on the scant bunch grass and started out on the trail. Had a chase after the horses and a cow until pretty well tired out—they seemed possessed with a spirit of getting away. There might have been Indians about which caused the uneasiness. Somewhat cloudy in the afternoon. After an uncomfortable drive arrived at Pinta Creek and camped. Eleven of us took the cattle off 1 1/2miles to feed and camped with them. The sheep remaining with the wagons at camp. Pleasant.

Saturday 22nd:

Had a cold night. On returning to the wagons in the morning found the sheep drivers had started off ahead, so we followed after them. Road rough—rocky and hilly. Crossed the summit of the southern rim of the Great Salt basin 54 days since we crossed the eastern rim. Overtook the sheep in a valley on Road creek and camped near Col. Hollister's train of 11 wagons, 154 cattle and about 4,000 sheep. 31 men employed. Cold all day. Overcoat, gloves and muffler in use. Had charge of the whole train. Frazer and Burnap being in the rear—their wagons and stock with us.

Sunday 23rd:

The Diary of Dr. Thomas Flint

Finding good feed for our stock we did not move out. Not so cold as yesterday, yet the altitude of the ridge made it colder than we had experienced for the month. Latitude about 37 1/2° North.

Monday 24th:

Coldest night yet experienced. Ice formed 1/2 inch thick. Drove 3 miles over the ridge and camped just at nightfall. I climbed a nearby peak from which I could see mountains in every direction but of less altitude than the one I stood upon. Warmer weather.

Tuesday 25th:

All hands in motion early. Right glad that we have passed out of Mormon territory. As for our individual selves we cannot complain of the treatment received since being in Brigham Young's worldly kingdom for we have been most kindly received and treated by Mormon church officials and members which we attributed to kindness returned for the relief given to their little trains that were robbed by the Indians on the Platt River. We were not robbed or molested to an amount more than a set of horseshoes. With other trains the treatment received was harassing in most every conceivable manner, particularly if they were from Illinois or Missouri. Fines were imposed by the authorities for every infraction of their regulations, real or fictitious— enforced by men with rifles on their shoulders, making their demands very emphatic. The Mormons that joined us were so much in fear of the "Destroying Angels" that they did not dare to venture away from the camp fire at night.

Road very rough and descending to the Santa Clara River— followed it down from where we struck it about a mile and camped.

No feed of much account. High bluffs on each side of the canon. Weather milder and pleasant.

Wednesday 26th:

Drove some 5 miles through thick willows, mud and water. Found an Indian corn field with the old stocks standing and some caches of large pumpkins. We took possession of the place and let the stock, cattle and sheep feed on the cornstalks but guarded them from the caches of pumpkins. An old Indian tried to make objections as nearly as we could make out from his pantomine gestures. In the afternoon a dozen Indians came to camp and we gave them some clothing and provisions in payment for our trespassing. The stock fared well however. Found 10 head of cattle got away in the willows and it took a long time to hunt them up.

One Indian who seemed to be big man of the tribe stayed in camp over night under guard. About midnight he stood up before the camp fire facing the east ridge of the mountain, made a lot of signs with his arms, blanket and body which we supposed had some meaning to the tribe on the ridge.

Thursday 27th:

Moved out quite early leaving our Indian visitor at the camping place where he breakfasted with us. On arriving at an open place about a mile out we had a count of the cattle and found one, a black cow, missing. Mr. Burnap and I started back on horseback to look for it. Had gone but a short distance when two Indians met us and one made an attempt to get on behind Mr. Burnap and he appeared to be willing to let him do so, but I spoke sharply to him to stop that kind of procedure for Mr. Indian would quickly have been the sole rider. At this stage of affairs some Indians drew up their bows with arrows ready to shoot, but perceiving that my revolver was in my hand they did not care to try conclusions. All this made it evident that they had the animal. We returned quickly to the train and reported. Six of us armed with rifles and shotguns besides our revolvers rode back to where the Indians had blocked the way but they had skipped. An old Indian by gestures warned us not to take a trail, a broad one leading to the summit of the ridge but we rushed up toward the top for we were sure the cow had been driven up there by finding her tracks. About half way up some Indians came driving the cow towards us pretending they had found her and asking by signs for a reward. We came upon the Indians before they could get the cow over the ridge out of sight, else we could have said goodbye to the pet black cow we had taken along from Illinois. On looking back when at our camping place the crest of the ridge was alive with Indians of all ages and sex who probably felt that they had lost a good breakfast. Drove on until tired with excitement and fatigue and camped in the canon. Pleasant.

Friday 28th:

Continued on down the canon. Trail crooked and full of brush. High bluffs on either side. No Indians in sight to trouble us for a mile or so when we came to a patch of thick brush full of them. They cut out some of our stock but they for some reason turned them back again. Camped at Camp Springs. Paid Indians two hickory shirts for bringing in a cow and one shirt for a calf. At night we killed a beef and gave the offal to the Indians, some 30 in number, who made way with every particle in short order. The chief took the hide. They came to camp almost naked and begged for everything they could get and when they obtained what they could, retired one side and reappeared dressed up in fine style in their clothing which was laid away in the brush.

Saturday 29th:

Started early for a 22 mile drive. Indians cross because we had got away before they dared to approach our camp as they knew full well that if they came near in the night they would be shot. We entered a narrow canon with abrupt rocky sides nearly perpendicular. From a cliff an Indian shot an arrow into one of Frazer's oxen. The arrow was pulled out leaving the head in the animal's paunch without seeming injury afterwards. About 10 miles drive we came out of the mountains into the Valley of the Rio Virjen. Camped with the sheep. Cattle driven on 6 miles to water. Found here the beehive cactus. Had to hunt for a yoke of oxen with a lantern to see their tracks. Found them about 10 o'clock at night. Pleasant.

Sunday 30th:

Started sheep at day break as there was ahead of us a long drive to the Rio Virjen for water and 2 miles down for feed. Found the cattle drivers who had driven ahead 6 miles yesterday trying to get their animals out of the thick brush into which they had strayed during the night. It was late at night when they came into camp where the sheep had stopped. Lost 2 head of the cattle. Camped 2 miles down river.

Monday 31st:

Started the sheep out on the trail. Ben, Frazer, Ed Wickersham and I turned back to hunt the 2 lost cattle. Saw a cow of Frazer's running along the ridge with Indian arrows sticking into her skin very thickly; the irritation crazed her and made her madly wild so we could do nothing with her. Going back a little further we found the tracks of the ox we had missed with Indian footprints following. We hurried on hoping to overtake them but at about 2 o'clock had to give it up. For variety gave chase to two Indians and they got away by dodging into a rocky gulch. We took the trail to get where our train would camp for the night. At sunset came upon Lewell with the sheep balked at a ford where they had been for six hours. Not a sheep would go into the water, although the water was not over 100 feet wide, so they were packing them over one at a time and their herd only about two thirds over. With our additional assistance soon got the balance across and it was nearly dark and cold. To make matters worse the cattle men . . . with the wagons that had our camping outfit, food, most of the bedding, etc. Jennings with his wagon stayed with the sheep as usual. Frazer, Wickersham, Ben and I started to get up to the cattle train and found them about 11 o'clock in camp with Col. Hollister's party. We got some food and blankets and returning got back at 2 o'clock in the morning.

November—Tuesday 1st:

Cattle remain in camp waiting for the sheep to get up to them. As there were 13 crossings to make ahead, I took charge of the sheep; men with the sheep weary and out of sorts, having had but little sleep. Some of them in dread of Indians did not go to sleep at all.

The first crossing we came to the sheep stopped, but I thought if we pressed them quietly the leading ones would start in to swim across therefore directed the shepherds to not make any noise and keep the dogs quiet also. In a little while the leader waded in when the men began to shout and the dogs to bark whereupon every sheep turned back to see what was up.

It was my turn to get mad apparently, so gave the men a good swearing for not obeying orders. They were grouchy, so when the next attempt was made they sullenly stood by at the places I put

90

them whilst I quietly worked the sheep, the outer ones crowding the ones at the edge of the water and in a short time being in the water they broke for the opposite side and there was no further delay. After that experience we had no further delay. Came up with the cattle about 4 o'clock. Glad to rest for the night. Was called to Hollister's camp to see a sick man. Found a case of fever, commonly called Mountain fever. Stopped over night as the patient was badly off. Mrs. Brown, the Colonel's sister having exhausted her skill on [him]. Pleasant weather.

Wednesday 2nd:

Returned to our camp and we moved out down the river some 5 miles and camped. Stock very troublesome to the guards. The grass too salty to satisfy their hunger. Pleasant. Here Frazer had another case of abduction. Dutch George induced his cook Isaac to leave the train with him.

Thursday 3rd:

Started out early and drove down river some 6 miles. Camped on some good bunch grass. The first fresh feed since striking this stream. Here we adopted a new course of treatment with the Indians by paying no attention to them unless they attempted to steal. It took a sharp watch to prevent that. They now stop but a short time in camp and only show themselves on the bluffs. Pleasant.

Friday 4th:

Stayed in camp for the benefit of the feed for the stock and the hands to slick up a little, kill vermin, etc. An Indian shot an arrow through a large fat black wether, killing. None of them in sight however. All in camp. Pleasant and quiet.

Saturday 5th:

Grazed stock in the morning and started but just at moving found Kit, a mare, missing, so Reuben and I stopped behind to look for her. Found she had been cut out from the band close by camp by a solitary Indian as shown by the tracks. We trailed it round through the little valley filled with low willows, but we could not come upon them, but found where we had been so close that the Indian had thrown her down to conceal it when near upon Mr. Indian and another place where it was driven in the bed of the creek where the water would wash away the tracks. Reuben was afraid of Indians and was a poor companion not dependable I found. On thinking it over it occurred to me that his prudence in not exposing himself was more commendable than my rashness but I felt that I could see as well as any Indian and could shoot just as quickly. It was getting near night and we started to overtake the train— found it in camp. The Indians were getting to be so troublesome that Hollister and ourselves concluded to declare war on them. Hollister having had an ox killed by them—so kept them off by taking a shot at them occasionally, not intending to hit.

Sunday 6th:

Got the sheep started on the trail and as the oxen were being yoked, Frazer by an unlucky blow on the head of one of his, felled him. Jennings cut his throat and beef was made of him. Then as we were counting the cattle, found **old Sorrel**, one of our horses missing. Found him nearby, the Indians being scared off before they could get out of rifle range with him. Drove a few miles to where Hollister's train was in camp and stopped near by.

Monday 7th:

By daylight we were in motion for we knew we had a very long steep hill to ascend, harder than any yet encountered on the route. Frazer had a wagon wheel broken, so had to lay by to repair it. The rest reached the top of the hill in safety. Wheel repaired. We leave the Rio Virjen which like the Santa Clara will not soon be forgotten by anyone having travelled along their banks. Off for The Muddy. Camped 10 miles out from top of hill. Dry grass for feed. A light shower moistened it a little.

Tuesday 8th:

After letting stock feed, started ahead again over a rough sharp gravelly trail. Pebbles like rasps. A great many sheep were left by the wayside by our's and Hollister's train, they having been worn out by the sharp gravel.

About two o'clock reached the streams rightly named Muddy water, generally 4 feet deep and mud deeper than water. Banks nearly perpendicular so we had to hunt quite a distance to find a place to get at the water. Camped to recruit for a few days.

Wednesday 9th:—Thursday 10th:

In camp. Indians on bluffs proffer friendship but we keep them out of rifle range by sending a bullet occasionally in their direction.

Friday 11th:

Moved up stream 8 miles. The Indians bounced in on the camping place immediately upon our departure to pick up any scraps that were left.

Saturday 12th:

Resting in camp getting ready for some hard and long drives ahead of us.

Sunday 13th:

Still in camp. Eleven head of cattle jumped off the steep bank where they could not get out and we had to drive them up stream about a mile—water and mud so deep that they had to swim from side to side and wade along the most shallow side of the stream. When we got them to a place they could climb out, some of them refused to make the attempt. Lewell and I had to get into the water behind them while others of the men had ropes around their horns tugging away to assist the animals. We were thoroughly tired, all hands, when we got out at 10 o'clock at night. Lost 11 sheep by poison of some kind but we could [not] discover what it was.

At this place a Mr. Livingstone from Missouri burned 25 wagons the year before and threw the iron into the deepest holes to keep it from the Mormons who had robbed or killed the mule teams; he had started out with the wagons for California, taking his men in some light wagons he had along with horse teams.

Monday 14th:

Started at midday to cross to the Las Vegas, 53 miles without water. Drove 9 or 10 miles and camped on some good dry grass.

Tuesday 15th:

At midnight had teams and stock put in motion. Drove until sunrise and took breakfast. Some feed for stock. Ben and Lewell left behind with sheep. Fed and drove along until 11 o'clock P. M. and camped in sight of the Las Vegas Creek.

Wednesday 16th:

Stayed in camp with cattle. Sheep arrived about noon, all standing the trip finely.

Thursday 17th:

Moved up the creek to the springs at its source some 4 miles. Pure water boiling up mixed with quicksand in which we sunk a rock fastened to a rope 13 feet. Clear for about 2 feet on top. About 20 feet wide and 30 long. Grass and weeds grow over the sides which seem perpendicular. Cattle step up to drink and slip in and have to be hauled out by the horns. Three of Frazer's had that experience.

Friday 18th—Saturday 19th:

In camp.

Sunday 20th:

Feed failing for the stock, we moved out a few miles and camped on dry grass without water. Separated Frazer's cattle from ours.

Monday 21st:

Moved on to Cottonwood Spring. 17 miles from the Vegas. Saw 4 antelope today. The first wild animals of any size that we have seen for a long time. A good spring. Poor feed.

Tuesday 22nd:

John Palmer left us here and joined a travelling train, that is, one that drove faster than we could. Started out after feeding the stock the best we could. Came to water in a ravine. Finding feed nearby camped about 6 miles from Cottonwood Springs. Used dry cactus for fuel. None other to be had. It answered the purpose well. Cold at night.

Wednesday 23rd:

Struck a range of mountains. The up hill grade and rough trail wearied our jaded stock. After making about 7 miles today camped near a spring. Poor feed. Cold night.

Thursday 24th:

Broke camp at daylight. Had a downhill grade about noon, came to feed where we nooned. Found an ox was missing from the herd. Lewell and I returned to the canon to look for him. Found some travellers at our last watering place. It was late and they were getting supper but did not offer us any. We had no blankets so we camped Indian fashion in a grove of cedars where there was dry wood for a fire, arranged a lot of boughs on the windy side so as to keep off the cold wind and with a lot more for a bed slept some but had to replenish the fire often. Had a cold night of it but the ground was dry.

Friday 25th:

Got some bread made of flour and water baked in a frying pan and some coffee of the Californians. They had nothing else.

Examined the country about there for the ox or signs of it but discovered nothing. Started to overtake the train. No water and no grub for the day. Travelled until about dark when Ben met us with water and food which was most needful to satisfy our cravings. We were heartily glad when he came in sight. Reached camp about 8 o'clock at Cottonwood Grove.

Saturday 26th:

Moved out on the old Spanish trail a short distance for feed and to rest awhile. Had a light shower in the morning with lightning and thunder.

Sunday 27th:

In camp all day. It took most of the day to water our sheep from two small holes of poor water but the best to be had.

Monday 28th:

Gave our stock what water we could get to and started for the main trail. Camped before we reached it. Had a sheep pierced with an Indian arrow this morning but did not see an Indian around and could find but one track freshly made.

Tuesday 29th:

Intended to have started out early but found that some of the cattle had strayed from the guard. Found them and started about sunrise. Crossed a high ridge and took our nooning. Crossed another and camped in a canon.

Wednesday 30th:

Arrived at Resting Springs. Anything but a resting place. Grass and water of the poorest quality. Hot at midday and cold at night. Came very near having an accident. White in taking a shot gun out of a wagon drew it toward him by the muzzle when the trigger caught and discharged it, the shot passing under the armpit close to his body. Time and time again the men had been cautioned not to take a gun that way.

December—Thursday 1st:

In camp. A party of California bound emigrants taking along the mail camped near us. Sent a letter to father by them to be mailed at San Diego. Started the sheep for the Amasgoshi creek or river.

Friday 2nd:

Moved out of camp early in the morning for the Amasgoshi. Travelled up and down a rough canon. About noon arrived at the Spring on the bank of that stream. High bluffs on each side. Water impregnated with alkali so strong the men did not need soap to wash their greasy shirts in it.

Saturday 3rd:

Started across the desert. Drove some 8 miles down the Amasgoshi and camped for noon. Trail sandy and soft. Used Hollister's old cart for fuel. Cattle weak from drinking the alkali water. Camped for the night at 11 o'clock P. M. Sheep did not come up to us.

Sunday 4th:

Waited for Ben and Lewell to come up with the sheep. When they came up, bid them "good morning" and left them with one wagon to make their way over the desert with the sheep as best they can. Arrived at Salt Springs about noon. Water of the springs too salt for our use. Left one cow unable to travel farther. Drove some 12 or 15 miles and camped near a dry lake.

Monday 5th:

Started at break of day and drove over a descending grade until noon. Rested and took lunch. Started out up hill. Rocky road. Entered a canon some 24 miles from Salt Springs. Drove until 10 o'clock and camped.

Tuesday 6th:

Had very little sleep last night. Drove 3 miles to summit between Salt Springs and Bitterwater Springs. On coming to a little grass, the first from Salt Springs turned out the stock for what feed they could get. Started the train after about two hours and I returned on the trail to bring up a mule cow that had fallen behind. Did not overtake the train with her and left her for next day and got into camp about 9 o'clock at Bitterwater Springs. Water very bitter but it answered very well when made into tea and could be drank clear by not stopping to taste it. No deleterious effects from it.

Wednesday 7th:

In camp all day. Hollister's first band of sheep came up in the afternoon. Jennings with his team from the sheep that were in the rear drive came to camp about midnight. Oxen nearly famished for

99

want of feed and particularly for water—a sad sight of brute suffering.

Tuesday 8th:

We were up nearly all night keeping guard over our cattle which kept straying away. Sent a relief wagon back to the men with the sheep. Ben and Lewell came up with them about 10 o'clock A. M. Hub Hollister came up with his flock just at night. Water scarce at best for so much stock.

Friday 9th:

Prepared some medicine for Hollister's men. Watered the stock the best we could and started out. Had to leave one ox behind, worn out. Ben and Lewell with the flock of sheep stopped to rest and feed the sheep on a little dry grass found left after the cattle had picked up what they could. They will start when they think best. We drove to a point of the bluffs and let the cattle pick what they could of the dry feed. Took our midday meal and started off again at sunset. Drove up hill about 7 miles and at 11 o'clock P. M. made camp.

Saturday 10th:

Off again at daylight. Cloudy morning. Rain in the P. M. Crossed summit of divide between Bitterwater Springs and Mojave River about noon. Cold. Drove down canon some 7 or 8 miles to grass at the outlet of the canon. Camped. Pleasant at night. Today's rain the first of any amount we have had on this drive from Salt Lake City.

Sunday 11th:

Pleasant again this morning. Arrived at the Mojave River as it is called. Water here but it sinks to rise again some several miles below and it is 11 miles up the wash to where the water is on top again. The desert is passed over with the cattle. Considerable grass here and we therefore camp to wait for the arrival of Ben and Lewell with the sheep.

Monday 12th:

I went up river 11 miles to where Frazer was camped to get some beef. Mr. Potter of Col. Hollister's train going with me. Got half of a steer and packed it back to our camps on two of the Colonel's horses for the use of the two camps. Had a headache today. Probably for want of good water and fatigue. The water here however is good comparatively.

Tuesday 13th:

Stayed in camp and out on the range with the cattle which had to be taken back on the trail some 2 or 3 miles for good feed on bunch grass. A raw, cold day. Snow squalls can be seen on the mountains.

Wednesday 14th:

After getting things righted about camp I packed my horse with water and cooked provisions and started to meet Ben and Lewell with the sheep. Met them some six miles out. They had used up all their water and food, hence it was a relief to them when I hove in sight. Some of the men had such a dread of the desert that they were beside themselves imagining they would perish from thirst before getting over the 40 miles of desert. Returned to camp and we were all again together.

McClanahan's train came up. They were out of flour. We were pretty short also. The Salt Lake flour did not spend nearly so well as the St. Louis.

Thursday 15th:

Resting in camp. Men loafing about the two camps or pitching horse shoes. Some are getting anxious and talk of starting off with packs on their backs for the settlements. Cold thin ice on still water.

Friday 16th:

Col. Hollister started for Los Angeles. Reuben Gill from our camp stampeded with him.

Saturday 17th:

Three men came in from the desert out of food except some meat from sheep we had left to die which they killed. Our boys took them in for the night before I came in from a tramp after some sheep that had strayed from the main flock. Some native Californians came into camp rather late and begged some bread.

Sunday 18th:

Found this morning that our lodgers had helped themselves or had been helped to a lot of provisions and had lit out. Lewell started after them, overtaking them found they had bread, beans, coffee and salt which they said had been given them by Press, a fellow we took in at Salt Lake City.

About 175 head of our sheep got mixed with the Hollister flock. Old Sorrel, a horse we bought in Terre Haute, died from alkali poison which had been weakening him for some time back.

Monday 19th:

Picked up our belongings and started on again. Drove about 7 miles to grass and camped for the night. Two of our horses gave us a chase of 3 miles ahead. They evidently scented water and went for it.

Tuesday 20th:

An Englishman, wife and child having lost their team and wagon came along footing it.
In the morning picked out the sheep that were marked from Col. Hollister's flock, 87 head of them. Drove to watering place. Rested awhile and went on about 4 miles and camped. The sheep did not arrive. The feed is poor. The last part of Turner's train passed.

Wednesday 21st:

I took a long walk ahead to examine the road. Marked stakes of an engineering party along the trail. Cattle scattered in the brush and it took half of the day to get them together. Drove past a bluff of the mountains and camped.
Col. Hollister took the Englishman, wife and child along with his train. Rain in the evening.

Thursday 22nd:

Started early in the morning to drive to water, then continued on until the stock began to show fatigue and camped on poor feed again. Light showers about noon. Pleasant and mild as May at sunset. Sierra Nevadas in sight. The pass must be near through which we are hoping to pass soon.

Friday 23rd:

Moved out and drove about 6 miles and camped away from timber. Weather getting cold. Snow on the mountains ahead in the road. Col. Hollister came into our camp about midnight cold and fatigued and stopped with his train which was behind us.

Saturday 24th:

After driving a short distance and watering, went about a mile from water on the road and camped on dry burr clover. This is an extensive range covered with wild grasses. Out of meat got some wild ducks for a stew and a mess of quail for Christmas dinner. Pleasant and cold. Built a big fire of dry cottonwood which gave a cozy look to the camp.

Sunday 25th:

Moved to the next watering place, a pool like the other water holes in the bed of the Mojave Thanksgiving day. Santa Claus made us a present of 7 sheep found here. Poor camping place. Dined on the quail shot yesterday. Remained in camp the rest of the day.

Monday 26th:

Started on again and after a short drive camped where the Mojave from here up is a steady stream. Some clover but rather poor feed.

Tuesday 27th:

Got to the last crossing of the road on the Mojave. Ducks, quail and rabbits contribute to our table. Weather cool. Bed of river full of green rushes.

Wednesday 28th:

Waited for Hollister's train to come up as we wanted to replenish our stock of flour—ours being all used up— which having been done we crossed the river here about 30 feet wide and 8 inches deep. Camped about 2 miles from river. Warm and cloudy weather. Lewell and I went out after rabbits. Didn't get any.

Thursday 29th:

Moved on towards the summit of the Sierras. Warm and pleasant. Green grass in places 2 inches high. Snow clad mountains on our right. Camped about 8 miles from summit as it is reported to us. Cloudy at night.

Friday 30th:

Crossed the mountains through the Cajon Pass. Gradual ascent from the Mojave. The descent steeper on south side. A little snow by the side of the pass. Camped in the brush on the side of the mountain.

Saturday 31st:

Down the canon to water about 25 miles from the Mojave and camped about a mile down the creek. Very little feed this side of. the pass.

Today closes the year 1853 and one year from the time we left San Francisco on the steamship Northener. In which time we have travelled by steamship 5,344 miles. Bv railroad 2,144 miles. I have [travelled] by steamboat on Mississippi and Missouri Rivers 1,074 miles. On horseback and on foot 2,131 miles, making a total of 10,693 miles on a direct line between the points reached. A month spent in Maine and 38 days collecting stock in Illinois.

Distances from Mountain Meadows, Utah, to Rim of Basin

To Spring	3	miles
Over divide to Santa Clara River	11	"
Down River crossing 10 or 12 times	16	"
To Spring	1 ½	"
To Feed south	2	"
To Rio Virjen	13	"
Down Rio Virjen crossing 12 or 15 times	30	"
Up Canon	7	"
And to top of hill steep	3	"
To Muddy Creek	13	"
Up Creek to Camp	3	"
	102 1/2	"
Thence to Feed	12	"
To Las Vegas from Muddy	38	"
Up Las Vegas to feed	3	"
From Las Vegas to Cedar Springs	7	"
To Rock Springs top of mountain	7	"
To Stump Springs	13	"

To Next Spring ½ mile right of road	3	"
To Rackton Springs	9	"
To Bitter Water and down to spring	2	"
To Salt Springs	13	"
To Middle of Desert, Bitter Springs	30 3/4	"
To summit of Divide (no water)	30 1/4	"
To Mojave River (no water)	17	"
Up Mojave River (feed and water).	51	"
To Cedar Grove (no water)	9	"
To Summit (Sierra Nevada) Mountains.	7	"
Down canon to spring	3	"
Down canon to spring	10	"
To Coco Mongo Ranch[19]	10	"
To Williams Ranch (Chino)	10	"
To Los Angeles	30	"
		417 1/2

---

[19] Cucamunga. [1923]

1854 – 1855 In California

1854—January—Sunday 1st:

Moved down Cajon Pass a short distance and camped.

By invitation took a New Year's dinner [with] Col. and Hub Hollister—Mrs. Brown, sister of Col. and Hub, made an extra effort in the culinary line to have a good dinner as the situation would afford.

Monday 2nd:

I took Jennings with his team and wagon, it being the lightest one in our train and went into San Bernardino for some groceries, etc. of which we had run out, particularly flour and tobacco. The latter article of luxury, those who used the weed were excitedly anxious for. Camped in the village of but a few houses, a store or two and grist mill.

Tuesday 3rd:

Refitted and returned to the train which had moved some 4 miles in the time I was in the town. Found that in the night a very heavy Norther had prostrated tents— wagons had to be anchored, cooking utensils that were at the camp fire scattered and a general dilapidated condition prevailed. Wind at night not very strong so we gathered up our scattered property and remained in camp. A cow that had a young calf was missing and as the calf was too young to walk it was put into a wagon when camp was moved— hence we supposed that she had returned some 5 miles to the camping place of the night before. Therefore Lewell and I started back to start to hunt her up. We were unable to find her that night so concluded to wait until morning as we did not want to return to the train without the animal.

Our next move was to find a place to sleep or to attempt it. Lewell had taken a single blanket along to use as a shawl and that was all we could have for a covering. We found a nice looking lot of leaves in a run which we got into like pigs but the cold air seemed to permeate every part of the pile and we could not build a fire without destroying our layout. About midnight we could stand it no longer so got out. The moon was bright and looking round discovered a slate ledge standing well above the surrounding surface in which there was a seam some 5 feet between the croppings and there was a lot of dry wood laying round and the wind did not strike in there. We made a fire, picked off the loose stuff and camped on the ground with the blanket over us. Had a good nap but was waked up by the cold when our fire burned down, replenished it again. Took another nap, during the sleep I dreamed that when we got up the cow was standing by the side of the ledge about 100 feet away and that I spoke to Bixby, calling his attention to it. On starting out, my dream came to pass exactly as I had dreamed.

It seemed that the cow had failed to find her calf and seeing the fire sought it, as accustomed to for a long time as headquarters during the long journey from Illinois.

We of course felt somewhat triumphant when we drove into camp and the cow seemed gratified to find her calf. Had she reason would probably have thanked us.

Wednesday 4th:

Packed up again. Made a day's drive and found ourselves in a different climate. Were told that there had been no wind there during the time we had to brace up to almost a blizzard. Had we known it we would have driven out of the wind belt.

Thursday 5th:

Drove past Coco Mongo vineyard and ranch. Camped. Friday 6th:
Arrived on the Williams Ranch, "the Chino"—helped ourselves to a fat calf as our animals could not yield any fat at that time. The moist land gave a good feeding ground which we let our stock utilize.

Saturday 7th:

Drove on towards Mission San Gabriel. Nothing out of ordinary course transpiring.

Sunday 8th:

Anniversary of the Battle of New Orleans; camped at the Mission.

Monday 9th:

A beautiful scene just at sunrise. There had been a light flurry of snow during the night which stuck to the orange leaves and to the fruit which when lighted by the clear morning sun made a most beautiful contrast of colors tropical and arctic.
Moved towards Los Angeles a few miles and camped for the remaining part of the winter.
The only incident out of the ordinary routine of camp life for two months was the birth of a son to Mr. and Mrs. Johnson.

Tuesday 10th:

Went into Los Angeles to fit out supplies for a two- months stay in camp before taking the coast route north.

From this time on we remained in the vicinity of Los Angeles. Bought out the remnants of two flocks of sheep.

White and Vial and — Borrowed $600.00 [from] Benito Wilson to pay above what we had on hand and Ben went to Mokelume Hill to get from acquaintances the money to Wilson.

The last part of March we started along the coast for Northern California. Drove through Santa Barbara, San Luis Obispo—San Juan Bautista to Santa Teresa Rancho, one Spanish League S. E. of San Jose, where we remained 14 months. While on that ranch sheared our sheep and sold the clip to Messrs. Moore and Folger at a bit a pound.

Purchased about 1,000 sheep of McMahon & Peters at $5.00 per head and brought them from near Petaluma. Sold 997 wethers for mutton at $16,000.00.

1855—July:

Moved to Monterey Co. for sheep feed.

In October bought the San Justo Rancho in the name of Flint, Bixby & Co., though with the understanding that Col. Hollister would pay for half of it. He being financially involved in Ohio took this way of arranging the purchase.[20]

---

[20] The firm was dissolved in 1861, Hollister getting half the property, the Flints and Bixby the remainder. Around 1875 Hollister sold his 20,773 acres for $370,000. See

https://en.wikipedia.org/wiki/William_Welles_Hollister

In time he returned to Ohio and settled in full with his creditors when a deed was made to Mrs. Lucy A. Brown, his sister, and after deeded by her to the Col.

The San Justo has been the home[21] place up to this time of Thomas Flint and family.

---

[21] According to Wikipedia, Flint's home today is the St. Francis Retreat. https://en.wikipedia.org/wiki/William_Welles_Hollister.

Notes by Sarah Bixby Smith

Dr. Thomas Flint, the author of this diary, was a graduate physician, who studied first at Waterville College in Maine and then completed his course and took his degree in Philadelphia in 1849.[22]

The young men who made this overland trip together were cousins through their mothers, Electa Weston Flint and Fanny Weston Bixby, daughters of Joseph and Anna Powers Weston of Madison, Maine. Llewellyn Bixby was the son of Amasa Bixby of Norridgewock, Maine. He and his brother, Amasa, Jr., were the first of the eight brothers and two sisters to come to California, all of whom ultimately made this state their home. Benjamin Flint came in 1849.

It will be noted that there is a break of a year and a half in the diary, covering the period spent in Volcano. This place was a characteristic mining town not far from Sutter's Mill, Mokelumne Hill, Hangtown and other places familiar to all who have read of the gold days in California. It was the point on the overland trail to which Kit Carson was accustomed to conduct emigrants, leaving them to find their own way from there on to their various destinations. The wheel marks of the old wagons are yet to be seen on the limestone rocks above the town.

---

[22] These Notes appeared at the end of the separate, pamphlet publication of Flint's Diary. Waterville College was renamed Colby College in 1867. However, Flint was not in Waterville to attend college – he was a medical student of Dr. Valorus P. Coolidge, convicted of murder in 1848, the conviction due in large part to Flint's testimony. Flint's degree was delayed for a year, according to the editor of the local newspaper, because of his involvement in Coolidge's trial, and uncertainty about his possible role in the crime.

The Diary of Dr. Thomas Flint

Within a few months of the arrival of Dr. Flint and Llewellyn Bixby, other brothers and cousins came until there were at least a dozen relatives in the district. All of these dabbled more or less in mining with the exception of Dr. Flint and Llewellyn Bixby, who after a week went into a butcher shop at first as employees, but very soon as owners. Benjamin Flint joined them, and with Mr. Charles Stone attended to the purchase of the beef in Southern California and fattened it for market on the Buena Vista Ranch, a very fertile piece of mountain meadow land six miles from lone.

Dr. Flint owned a very accurate pair of scales, possibly apothecary scales, and as the partners soon won a reputation for honesty the miners in the vicinity came to them for the weighing of their gold dust. Doubtless the payment for this service was an important factor in the accumulation of the capital for their stock-buying trip to the East.

The diary closes with a note as to the purchase of the San Justo Ranch. This remained headquarters so long as the firm lasted, and was the home of the three men and their families until the later seventies when the Ben Flints moved to San Francisco and the Llewellyn Bixbys to Los Angeles, leaving the Doctor's family at the home place. The ranch house was a large modern one built by the three men in 1862. It contained three separate sets of living quarters, but a community parlor, office, dining room and kitchen.

The flocks increased and the wool business was profitable, especially during the years of the Civil War. In order to provide additional grazing land the firm bought several ranches, among them the Huero Huero and a San Joaquin somewhere in Central California.

They entered the southern part of the state in 1866 when they purchased from Don Juan Temple the Rancho Los Cerritos. Mr. Jotham Bixby, a younger brother of my father was put in charge with the privilege of buying a half interest, which he did three years later from his share of the profits from the wool. Later the firm acquired interests in the Rancho Los Alamitos, the Rancho Palos Verdes and the southern Rancho San Joaquin, which later they owned with Mr. Irvine for a time, but which they sold to meet the exigencies of a situation of financial stress occasioned by a combination of disasters,—a country-wide season of "hard times," a dry year, an epidemic among the lambs and an unfortunate mining venture.

This firm was primarily interested in land and wool and by their importation of fine Spanish merino sheep materially improved the quality of the California product, but they branched out into several other lines. From 1869 to 1877 they operated the Coast Line Stage Co., which carried the mail, Wells Fargo Express and Passengers between San Francisco, Los Angeles and San Diego.

Flint, Bixby & Co. were the first in California to undertake the manufacture of sugar from beets and established a large factory at Alvarado about 1872, which they later moved to Loquel. This plant shut down in the early eighties because at that time the process of making beet sugar had not been developed to the point where it was possible to make the product altogether attractive to the consumer.

This firm was dissolved after the death of Llewellyn Bixby in 1896, the Flints retaining the northern* properties and the Bixbys the southern. Mr. Benjamin Flint died in 1881 and Dr. Flint in 1904.

Dr. Flint's eldest son, Thomas Flint, Jr., was at one time Lieutenant Governor of California, and Benjamin Flint's son, William Flint, has been in the State Senate. Llewellyn Bixby's son of the same name is a responsible business man of Long Beach, California.